# Be Quiet & Eat Your Chicken Feet!

Humorous Insights Into Family World
Travel From A Half Crazy Father

R. K. Jepson

First Printing, 2015

ISBN 978-0692568521

Back On The Road Publishing
League City, Texas 77573
www.RTWFamilyTravel.com

*Dedicated to the special woman*
*and little ladies in my life,*
*who are also my favorite travel buddies.*
*I love you.*

# Table Of Contents

# Introduction

Humorous Insights

# Me and My Four Very Vocal Travel Mates

Sometime ago, in a mental galaxy far, far, really far out there, there was a tall chap... let's call him Richard.

Richard, that's me, decided it would be really cool to travel the world. See foreign lands, eat exotic foods, do strange things, and live life on the high-side... you know, all seemed to be a dream. Of course, give me a half-baked idea and I'm sure to slam it back into the oven until it's at least mostly burnt, or the smoke excites the neighbors into calling the fire department.

My wife, Cindy, didn't think the idea was half-baked, she just thought I spent too much time in my home town of Las Vegas inhaling the down drafts of the nuclear testing facility. Unfortunately for her, she actually grew up in the trade winds of the test site and it's her that ended up marrying a lunatic like me. So who is the crazier person, the person doing crazy things or the other person following that crazy person? Thanks Ben Kenobi for that one.

So I designed this whole plan on traveling the world, but Cindy didn't want to go. Communism, wars, pirates, thieves, and lurking nuns all scared her. Who could blame her? She had a point – with the millions of nameless victims of commie nuns stealing luggage in war-torn, and pirate countries. I reassured her that we weren't going to Philadelphia, and she was then fine with the whole plan – as long as we had travel insurance, had a renter for the house, updated all our vaccines, secured all of our medical needs, and donated a large sum of money to the Supreme Being.

No problem. Check, check, check, check, and big check to Supreme Being.

Ready to go! Load 'em up kids, we have nothing to lose!

We packed up our travel crap (much more than we needed) and took off to the great unknown, which so happened to be San Antonio, where we lost our expensive Canon camera due to commie, window smashing, pirate thieves. I knew I should have written a bigger check to the Supreme Being… or to my Mafioso insurance company.

Hey, no problem, we called the San Antonio Police to help us track down the rascals.

"Good luck with that!" Not an exact quote from the police, but the meaning was the same. Oh well, it was only Father's Day and all. Not a bad day for Day One.

Honestly, it was probably the worst day of the entire year. Sure my three daughters planned how to overthrow my travel dictatorship about every other day (anarchy is hard to organize on an allowance), but for the most part, the trip was golden… in memories and price.

Now after almost a year of traveling, we can say we circum-navigated the globe… from Argentina, to Costa Rica, Samoa, New Zealand, Australia, Singapore, Malaysia, Thailand, Cambodia, China, Italy, and the United Kingdom. LAX, to LAX, to LAX.

It all adds up to over 60,000 miles of planes, trains, boats, bicycles, campervans, cars, taxis, ferries, scooters, and Tuk-Tuks.

Miraculously we lived to tell the tale. And oh what a tale it is. Though, we can't discuss the trip in its entirety as some things should remain unknown to the public, some things should stay secret for my pride's sake, and some things you just wouldn't believe if I told you – though most people don't believe half of what I swear is the gospel truth, sworn on my own copy of the NanoBible (if you have no idea what a NanoBible is, I will show you my own microscopic copy. Oops, I lost it).

My only wish is that everyone, in some point in their lives, embraces the same insanity of global travel. Not only do you become one of the few out there with international exposure, you too can partake of fine foreign foods such as chicken parts stew. My kids call it "Walkie-Talkie," … a local delicacy of chicken beaks, chicken feet, and various other inedible chicken parts. Parts that walk and talk are always the hit of the party.

Join us in our journey. Sit down, sit back, and eat up!

# Chapter 1:  United State of America:

# The U. S. Of Ehhh Wait A Minute!

Humorous Insights

# Everything is Bigger in Texas

Have you ever tried to drive from one end of Texas to the other?

*Of course you haven't tried, because you're smart. You have already realized that Texas is too stinkin' huge to simply drive through. You are intelligent enough to fly from one end to the other and save hours of your life.*

HEY, what are you doing to my computer? Are you writing in my book? Get off of that!

Sorry, my wife is was typing that. I think she is trying to teach me a lesson on long-distance traveling in confined spaces. Well, she is correct, Texas really is big, but she is dead wrong on whether it's smart to drive from one end of Texas to the other.

Sure, it takes hours of driving. Sure, the kids start counting the dead armadillos. Sure, we changed the oil twice by the time we got out of Texas. Let me remind her though that Texas is worthy of the drive.

Example: Schlitterbahn

Where else can you go that is constantly rated the best waterpark in the USA. This waterpark has so many rides and things to do, you wear out your swimsuit from all the slides.

*Correction: He just hasn't bought a new swimsuit for fifteen years, and it's at the end of its natural lifecycle.*

Hey, are you typing again? Get off of there! This is my book! What did she type? Hey, I love that swimsuit. And I've only had it for a couple years... err... decades. It's sentimental.

Another example of how big Texas is: the state capitol

The Texas state capitol building is 302 feet tall, almost 15 feet taller than the US capitol building. Now that's big. That's Texas big.

What? Louisiana's is taller? How tall? Well, we're talking about Texas here, not Louisiana. And you can drive through Louisiana on a quarter tank of gas. I'm telling the story here.

Yet another example of Texas big: historical-figure statues

Have you ever seen the statue of Sam Houston off of I-45, just North of Houston? Holy-Guacamole! If you drive by it, you cannot help but see it. That would be a tragedy to miss. Of course, now that I think of it, it may be big enough that you could see it while flying over it. Texas big!

Last example: gas stations

If you didn't drive through Texas, you wouldn't get the experience that is almost cult-like. I'm talking about Buc-ee's convenience stores. You find them mostly in East Texas, but my point is that they have a few huge stores. One store is in New Braunfels, Texas – close to Schlitterbahn (*that's where he bought a new swimsuit...* stop it Cindy!). It is 68,000 square feet of convenience store. The largest one in the world. That's Texas big.

This Buc-ee's location has some eighty-three toilets. Why bring up the bathroom? Simple. It is the exact opposite of gas station restrooms. They are so clean; they leave mints on the urinals. That's what they say anyway, and the one I tasted was perfectly fine (Ouch! Stop it, Cindy!). Buc-ee's was named the cleanest bathrooms in the USA by Cintas. That designation has to be worth something.

So if you want to drive through Texas, be prepared for everything being big. *Big hairdos, big BBQ, big trucks, big football stadiums, big smiles, and big, long, "my butt is asleep" drives with occasional stops at Buc-ee's.*

Cindy, stop typing in my – wait, it was a big, long drive – Texas big. OK, you win.

Want a mint?

# Go Visit Concordia, Kansas

Every major, long-term travel writer will tell you that an open travel log, free from confinement and structure, creates unique and fresh experiences. When you have time to explore and dig deep, you uncover a world of wonder that you easily would have passed otherwise.

Well, I believe that you don't necessarily need to blow like a leaf in the wind; instead, a semi-planned route and agenda, especially with kids, can make great vacations and trips. The problem is people over-plan and over-book their time. This scenario makes for a stressed out group when times and schedules don't pan out as planned, and a stressed out group of kids will turn a pleasant picnic into a mud wrestling fight to the death.

Bad for moral, but great for public entertainment.

There is something else to be said about loose schedules. When things go wrong, you have time and mental clarity to deal with the issues. Let's make up a problem... say your dog, a Yorkie, is traveling with you. He won't eat, pukes all day, and looks horrible. Well, if you were on a tight tour schedule, you would be so wound up, you could spin yourself a hole to China. If you are flexible, though, you could find yourself staying in Concordia, Kansas.

Concordia is on the map, but is off the map. You can walk from one side of downtown (yes, there is one) to the other side in five minutes (I'll time you first). No surprise that there is a vet in the area — one of those good vets, that can care for dogs, cats, cattle, horses — but don't even think of bringing in poultry (That's what the sign said anyway, something like "Keep your $%@# poultry to yourself. Big Bird Sucks! Have a good day!").

When you find yourself in a small, country, Kansas town, with a *lot* of time on your hands, because your wimpy dog is a pansy and gets all sick and pucks every ten miles and AUGHH... er, I mean, that poor, little guy is suffering. I feel horrible. Anyway, with so much time, you have no reason not to check out their two main museums: The Cloud County Historical Museum and the Orphan Train Museum.

But let's not forget lunch. This is Kansas, and there is barbecue to eat! Ask anyone. If you can catch someone walking or running or riding their electric scooter across the highway (this isn't funny, Grandma could have gotten killed by that semi!), and they will tell you to go to Heavy's BBQ.

I am fanatical about Texas barbecue, but this Kansas grub was great! They had a different flare to the potato salad (more mayonnaise and less mustard) and coleslaw (horse radish bitter), but I really enjoyed the food and experience. Being greeted by the owner, to me, was fantastic, a hard reminder that so many restaurants and service-related industries have lost contact with their customers.

OK... back to these museums. Let's discuss the Cloud County Historical Museum. Yep, that's the one — yes-sir-ee, it has the three huge, iron wheat stalks in the front lawn. Who has massive, metal wheat stalks on their lawn? Had to get a picture of this crap — friends back home wouldn't have believed me on this one.

There was this gentle, elderly woman who walked the entire museum explaining things to our family (this was a must as our three girls were much more interested in her than their parents). I believe she was just waiting there for weeks for someone to pop a tire and end up in her museum. Probably threw a small handful of nails on the freeway to get people to come to the museum during their four-hour wait to fix the tire. Did I call her "gentle?"

Summary: full bi-plane, fire brigade cart, two Ford Model T's, World War II uniforms, original telephone switch boards (with full commenting on how it functioned since our tour guide volunteer actually worked as an operator years ago), broom manufacturing, and German POW camp memorabilia (they had 5,100 prisoners north of town, and many of those prisoners decided to not return back to Germany after the war). How cool is that?

So next time, leave your travel agenda open, your mind free for exploring, and go visit Concordia! You may be surprised to find yourself taking pictures next to big, steel wheat stalks while your wimpy...er, sick dog gets better.

# 50 States... Phew!

It all started twenty-five years ago when my parents decided to drive around the United States in our motorhome. I probably wouldn't have cared or even noticed how many states we had physically been to, but my Dad bought a blank United States sticker map and placed it right next to the door of our "house on wheels."

This sticker map was of all fifty US states, one of those that you place a colored sticker from each of the states you have been. It leaves all of the unvisited states blank and dull. With each new state, we kids would love to see the new colorful addition to our wall of pride. We even drove an hour out of the way to make it to the Kentucky state line, take a picture, and then turn around and drive off in the opposite direction. Coloring the country became just as important as the trip itself. It became an obsession. How was I going to make it to all those uncolored states?

College added Montana and Idaho – I mean you have to see Yellowstone and the Tetons once in your life.

Graduate school added Louisiana – Wow; we can actually rent a boat to paddle around the alligators? That's so cool, don't tell Cindy... She'll freak out that I'm taking Amber.

First job... man, I have to get out of West Texas – I'm too far from everything.

16

Second job... OK, going to other countries is really fun, but I'm still not coloring that darn sticker map!

Third job... Honey, I love you soo much... let's go to Hawaii! Great, I've already bought the plane tickets. Hey, I've always wanted to go to the Redwoods and Vancouver, let's go camping! (That gets Oregon and Washington. How in the world am I going to get Alabama and Mississippi?)

Alaska... sure I'd love to go on a fishing trip to Alaska, but why don't you go Cindy – it's your brother's idea – OK, since it's a guy's trip, I'll go. (hehehe)

Move to Houston... Wow Cindy, there is a Speech Pathology Conference in New Orleans, you should go. OK kids, Mom is occupied all day. We're going on a car ride, just till we see the beach in Alabama!

One state left... North Dakota. Why does it have to be North Dakota? When you live in Southeast Texas, it is really hard to make it to a state like North Dakota. Think about it, what good reason do I have to see a state so far away and I hate to say this, with not that much for me to see? I'm not a hunter, and I really don't like cold weather. I'll have to think about this one.

The SOLUTION: Mount Rushmore! Cindy has always wanted to see Mt. Rushmore. We need to see family back west, why not make a pre-trip trip?

Honey, I know it's a bit out of the way – it'll be fun though! The kids love to see the open road even though it'd be 3000 miles of it.

So we spent a half day driving to North Dakota from Keystone, South Dakota – open plains, beautiful weather, and rolling hills. When we got there, it almost didn't seem possible. Twenty-five years of my life in this crazy, entertaining ambition to see all fifty of my country's states, and here it is in the farm land of southwest North Dakota. I better walk a bit farther into the state just to make sure; I don't want any technicalities.

As we drove back to Mount Rushmore, with the USA country sticker map fully colored in blues, reds, oranges, and yellows in my mind, all I could think about was what to do next. The European Union, South America, the old Russian Republic? I wonder if they have a sticker map of those places.

# End of Our USA Tour

After driving 5,820 miles across a lot of the United States, you would think you would be tired of driving. Well, you would be right, but it was all worth it.

Cindy and I know that leaving behind family would be difficult, especially since we would not see them for a year (of course my younger brother, Ellis, throws rocks at me whenever he sees me... hmmm?). A year is a long time not to see the people you care about. So for the last month, we spent time with family in Las Vegas, Nevada, and around Utah.

Cindy and I figured that if we would be gone for a year, we needed to have about a year's worth of time with family, and after the happy goodbyes we got upon leaving, I believe we succeeded. My four-month old niece even puked on me to say "get lost." I could hear the fireworks going off only minutes from leaving my brother's home.

The great thing about visiting family is that after a few hours of chatting about the good old days, they're bored of staring at you and say things like "let's go do something," or "how about going somewhere," or "did you have that pimple on your nose yesterday?"

Cindy's sister lives in Price, Utah. This area is famous for dinosaur bones and tracks good enough that there is a national park close by

19

solely about dinosaurs. So after staring at each other for a few hours, we went to CEU/USU's Prehistoric Museum.

Now I have been to several Natural History Museums, and seen some impressive stuff, but for the low entrance fee and exhibits on hand there, I rank the museum as a "must see." Not only does it have a mammoth skeleton, a great Ute Indian display, but the allosaurus and Utah-raptor skeletons are fantastic. And for the kids, it was paradise. Kids simply love dinosaurs. I don't know exactly why, but they do. They go crazy every time they see one. It's "AUUGGHH! Stop the $@#$% car, it's a dinosaur museum!" crazy, and with home schooling, to have them learn something educational while they have fun doing it... priceless!

From Price, we ended up in Las Vegas. I grew up in Las Vegas, so for us going there tends to be the exact opposite of what you see on TV. We don't go gamble all of our money in casinos, or run butt-naked through the streets screaming profanities, or eat buffet food like it is some game of who pukes first. Las Vegas is simply the place I grew up and became the weird person I am today – err – where I developed my unique personality (that sounds tons better). I even asked Cindy not to be married in my home town just because I didn't want to have to always explain our marriage wasn't a drunken weekend fiesta. Vegas is just different for me because I don't go there to be a tourist; I visit Vegas to sit in my family's living room and tell each other the interesting things that occurred since the last time I was in their living room.

But something happens after you've discussed your dog's hygiene problems. Magically, you go do things ("Enough chit chat, I'm getting sick listening to you. I need some fresh air."). Like...

- Bowling a score of 200! I swear I didn't Photoshop this picture and I have the witnesses to back me up.

- Seeing the Nevada Natural History Museum; The Egyptian Section was by far my favorite and probably one of the best in the USA.

- Going to see the free fountain show at the Bellagio. It was hotter than John Hardy's Atomic BBQ sauce, but the show was cool. It only lasted about five to seven minutes, but it was worth the drive and ten dollars of drinking water I bought afterwards. Vendors must be from the Treasure Island Casino. Pirates!

- Then the king attraction for families lost in Vegas – Bellagio's Botanical Gardens – a wonder of wonders. How they keep such a beautifully decorated garden, one that looks like you've been shrunk to the size of a gnat's bottom, is phenomenal, especially since it is in the middle of the blasted desert.

So if you find yourself sitting around your family's living room and your extended family is starting to wish you had a motorhome that they could throw you into and then roll you down a mountain, a great alternative is seeing the local sites. It always seems that you miss out on the sites anyway, and you can have meaningful conversations along the way... discussions like "Wow, that made me feel like the size of a gnat's butt" or "King Tut had a lot of crap, didn't he?"

Either way, you've driven a gazillion miles to see family, what's another ten to see something amazing (besides that pimple on your nose, of course).

# Chapter 2: Argentina:

# Sorry, No Hablo Whatever The Crap You're Yelling!

Humorous Insights

# Why Not Argentina?

It is interesting how you get questions that sometimes you can't fully answer, like for example: why did you go to a Hannah Montana concert alone? Or, where do babies come from Daddy? Or more appropriately, why did you go to Buenos Aires?

OK, for the record, I have never been to a Hannah Montana concert, but I am willing to bet there are those out there wondering how I knew you went!

Why Argentina? Why not! That answer really doesn't address the question, but sometimes you can't fully respond to a question that you haven't fully developed the answer for. Confused? Let me pontificate.

I had always wanted to go to South America — it just sounded fun in my mind for the following reasons. It's far enough away from the USA that you are intriguing to the locals. They mainly speak Spanish or Portuguese (I've studied Spanish and my two brothers speak Portuguese. It would be nice to know what they are saying when I know they are talking about me). South America is also culturally different from what I was raised with — schools, sports, eating, entertainment, hobbies. I imagined it would be a blind-folded, head-first dive into a cultural pool of awe.

So why Argentina, why not Peru or Colombia or Chile or Brazil?

That is where it all gets a bit foggy. I should have had a stellar reason for flying my family of five to one of the southern most cities in the world (Cape Town, South Africa and Sydney, Australia are about the same longitude), right? Well I do have a stellar reason and the reason is...

OK, so I really didn't have one. What are you, the Spanish Inquisition? Does anyone need more than Tango, a rich history, and empanadas? There was a gut instinct that Buenos Aires would be fabulous. We simply just had to go and prove it to ourselves.

Week one in Argentina was just that, getting to know why we went there and here are some of the reasons:

- **Architecture** - The houses in San Telmo, downtown near Plaza De Mayo – all of them – are works of art. Builders don't make exteriors anymore with the flare you see in Buenos Aires. Repeatedly, you hear that Buenos Aires is the Paris of South America; from what I've seen, I believe it. It is so much fun to marvel at doors with gargoyles, balconies with delicate ironwork, and floors with intricate tile. San Telmo, where we stayed, is bursting with elaborate facial work. If you visit the area around Casa Rosada or Avenida de Mayo, then you will understand what I mean.

- **Empanadas and Parrillas** - It's entertaining to make food a reason to visit a country, but people do this all the time – think of Italy. Empanadas are small bread pies filled with beef, chicken, or vegetables. They are everywhere and it seems that no two panaderias (bakeries) have the same recipe. They are fun and tasty meals that the girls loved. The parrillas (grills) are world renowned. Bife de lomo (a fillet type steak) and Bife de chorizo (a ribeye type steak) are the standard and delicious. Argentine cuisine is good enough that Cindy and I couldn't resist scheduling a cooking class. No international incidents but there were coughing and smoke involved.

- **Sports** - Websites tell you not to discuss sports, soccer in particular, with Argentinians. They mention that there is too much emotional connection with their personal teams and you might upset them. Well, that sounds a little entertaining to me. Put that on my list of things to do to get killed. Now, I do understand this whole theory though – we did see the Bombonera, the Boca Junior's stadium on the bus tour of the city we went on. It is big and colorful and a place that I would really like to see a soccer match. So, I have that on my list of ways to kill myself also. Doesn't it sound like fun?

- **Tango** - This dance originated with the slave population, through the Italian immigrants, to Paris and back, and then became a national pastime. I hate dancing. I look like a redwood tree on stilts trying to stomp on a cockroach. I look silly and feel stupid, but Cindy loves to dance. So, in an effort to score some *major* points and transform myself from a stiff tree into a crazed chimp on stilts, I took some lessons (realistically, one, but it felt like fifty).

So, that's it. That is why we came to Argentina. And believe it or not, I didn't fall off of a hundred year old balcony, choke on a burnt empanada, break a leg while dancing, or get beat up for wearing the wrong jersey. Success!

Having shared why Buenos Aires is worth the flight price still doesn't explain why I didn't choose Peru or Brazil. My response: Those are trips in the future... but don't tell Cindy until I create a good reason why we should go.

# Argentina Metro Magic

Most big cities around the world have metro or subway systems. Personally, I love Metros, mainly because I'm cheap and they're cheap – match made in heaven. Not only are metros inexpensive, they are also a convenient way of getting around. Most importantly, above all other reasons or rationales to ride the glorious metro, you go because it is one of the finest arenas of human interaction and pure… how do you say, bizarro-land.

Let's chat a bit about Metro etiquette.

First, no one wants to talk to anyone, everyone is perfectly content being left silently alone. Pretty sad really. You have hundreds of people in a confined space and the last thing on Earth they would rather do is shoot the breeze with a stranger. You get on the subway in New York City and people have three tier strategies to avoid eye contact or conversation. I know of people who pretend to listen to their iPods on the Metro so that someone will have to interrupt their false music entertainment to talk to them. This is serious anti-talkie-to-somebody effort.

Next, no one wants to touch anyone. Was that you touching my leg? Where's my wallet – I bet he was going for the wallet! Can't you see I stood in the corner so that I wouldn't have to stand next to someone like you? It's human-toucha-me-phobia!

So, when we discovered the Metro in Buenos Aires, I was perfectly aware that these rules were well established internationally, as an Italian once told me, "Non sai la legge internationale di metro? Ho capito, sei Americano!" (Translated: You don't know the international Metro laws? Oh, I understand, you're American!)

Somehow, and I don't know what I was thinking, I forgot to properly instruct my girls on this basic human practice because the first time they got on, they thought it was Disneyland.

The girls *had* to stand. While every Argentinian was clawing for a seat, they wanted to stand. Why? Because when the train banked sharply to the left and right, they giggled and laughed at the top of their lungs. They also talked really loud, they hogged the door way, and they loved to stare directly at anyone who wanted no attention at all. Basically, completely unorthodox metro behavior.

So, what did I do? Nothing! Why? It was good entertainment for everyone!

Now something else about Argentinians and the subway: They are crazy polite. But let's hold that thought while I explain that I have never seen capitalism like I have seen it on the metro. Singers, beggars, vendors... I wouldn't be surprised if one day I'll see stock traders doing side business on the Linea A.

The singers. Some are horrible; like, "here's 10 pesos to make the screeching stop!" Some are fantastic; for example, "I'm so proud of my son and his singing career. I knew all that money I spent on lessons would someday pay off!" The crazy thing is that when they are done, everyone claps. Did you hear me, they CLAP! The performer could totally suck, and they clap! These are the same people that don't want to talk to the Dalai Lama sitting next to them, but they will applaud the rubberband concerto that just wrapped up.

The vendors. Bedlights, tissues, bus maps, candy, DVDs of movies still in the movie theater – you almost don't have to go to the store they sell so much stuff here. Now the kicker, they walk around and leave things on your lap, walk off so that you can inspect the superb quality and low price, and come back a minute later to collect the merchandise or your money (sweet, don't have to go out tonight, I have the newest DiCaprio movie!). They leave the goods on your lap and Argentinians politely leave them there while waiting for the vendor to return. If this was tried in New York, the dude would quickly distribute the high end pencil sharpeners to everyone, turn around afterwards, and find that no one seems to have the merchandise still on their lap and they all swear that they have never seen you before... robbed! But not in Argentina. Mama told me to never hose a metro vendor – that will send you straight to the Diablo!

Now *that* is good manners.

So, the next time you want to upend local traditions on your neighborhood subway, take your kids with a box of high-end electric toilet bowl scrubbers. They will either surf the whole ride, giggling the entire time, or make you a buck or two while learning their first lessons on capitalism.  Either way, it will be a hilarious ride for you – just remember your camera.

# The Richard Jepson Reality Bus Tour

If you know me really well, you will know I love the TV show Seinfeld. I have seen each episode a countless number of times. Cindy used to ask me all the time why I was watching the re-runs so often (it drove her crazy that I was ONCE AGAIN watching Seinfeld when there were other options). The answer was simple – it made me laugh, and who doesn't like to laugh, especially when things really sucked at work that day. Ex: "You want me to do that? But that will cost you a lot of money and cause me a lot of pain? OK, you own the place!"

Well, I bring this up because there is an episode on Seinfeld where Kramer (a goofy main character) is running his "J Peterson Reality Bus Tour." It's so funny, Kramer has to haul all these muffin bottoms, hehe, to the dump, haha, along with a bunch of tourists but he can't and ends up driving for hours HAHAHA! (wipe eyes, suppress more giggles). Anyway, we drove on a 17 hour bus ride to Northern Argentina, to the border of Paraguay, Brazil, and Argentina (called Tres Fronteras). The city is called Puerto Iguazu and is near Iguazu Falls (the main reason we went). This bus ride was my Reality Bus Tour of Argentina.

Seventeen hours sounds like a long bus ride; really, it is not as bad as a 19 hour bus ride (the one back to Buenos Aires - love rush hour). It is not a laugh a minute but it is quite interesting. You eat, sleep, drink, read, write, and watch the world go by. They play movies and all in all, the time goes by pretty fast. The only complaint I have is that your legs feel like they have been through a medieval rack machine.

As for the bus, it was a double decker with chairs on the bottom and top floors. The chairs folded down for sleeping, such as 120, 160, or 180 degrees. We chose the 160 degree chairs, called "semi-cama" in Spanish (the 180 deg chairs cost more and we didn't think it was worth it), so they're almost beds, just not completely. I think I would have needed two chairs laid flat to even come close to being perfectly comfortable. The upper floor had a great view and I am so glad that we chose it.

So, leaving Buenos Aires for a few days was bitter-sweet. Bitter because I really did like Buenos Aires and we were set up quite well. Sweet because it was a new adventure and we needed one as things were getting a little too routine. Buenos Aires is a massive city and to be in the center and see the outskirts was a treat. There were houses, companies I recognized (Bayer, Caterpillar, Phillips), big shopping centers and cinemas. I was beginning to think we were in America.

When I woke up the next morning, on the bus and far from Buenos Aires, I was immediately reminded that I was nowhere near America. Houses were made of tin sheets, people were bathing in the river, water tanks lined all the homes, and there was no central planning with any of the cities and towns we went through. It appeared that most people were content working outside with government work (making bridges / fixing roads) or running the small shops they owned (fruit / grocery / bread / pressure gauges).

OK, side note here, just because it always blows my mind. Specialty stores outside the US are exactly that, specialty stores. You go to the tire store for tires (not that weird), you go to the bread store to get bread (don't see these in the USA that often anymore, unfortunately), you go to the firefighter store for all your firefighter needs (how many 'bomberos' are out there to support a whole store?), and a pressure gauge store for pressure gauges (like each bathroom faucet has one to get the perfect pressure in psi). However, I bet you will get the best pressure gauge service in the world from this pressure gauge store dude: "No, only an idiot would use that one, you need an Ashcroft Type 1279 Duragauge – that will get the job done right!" I bet your Walmart couldn't help you determine which gauge you need like a pressure gauge store owner!

The ride back to Buenos Aires was an education in how Argentina handles public safety or border protection. At 10:30 PM, our bus was stopped and searched by the Argentine Military (specifically the Gendarmeria - or border guards). We were asked for our passports and randomly had our bags searched. As a clarification, we never crossed any borders on our trip; this must have been for anyone who swam across a border or came across somehow illegitimately. They let us move on, no problem, until 2:30 AM when we were woken again by another Gendarmeria post. This time, one of our passengers was asked to get off the bus – I believe it had something to do with the 30 inch long machete he was toting in his knapsack. At that point, I felt a lot safer having the military doing double checks on our bus. In fact, I gave the lady behind me a much more thorough look over. Who knows, she could be packing a grenade in one of those... never mind. Not a good train of thought. Anyway, the man got back on our bus after about 10 minutes of questioning, but I have no idea if he still had his machete. Amazingly, Cindy and the girls slept through the whole thing.

My Richard Jepson Reality Bus Tour was one for the books. Surprise, misconceptions, fear, excitement, and a lot of deep reflection. It made me realize, once again, one city can't possibly describe an entire country any better than a peach pit depicts what a peach tastes like. The drive gave me a sense of wealth and complete poverty. It reminded me that there are different ways of accomplishing almost anything you do, from house building, to car maintenance, to selling goods. It was pure "Reality" and it didn't even have the muffin bottoms to accompany the 18 hour drive, but it did have a ton of Flan.

# Argentina - Why I Can't Wait To Go Back

It was rainy and cold the day we left Argentina – it was still winter there. Spending a month in Argentina was just about right for me. I had met my lifetime quantity of stepping in sidewalk dog crap and I had exhausted my neck muscles having to duck going into our apartment bathroom (Question: Why was our living room door 14 feet tall and our bathroom door 5 and a half feet tall? I shouldn't even bring up the teal wall paint!).

Why then, am I so excited to eventually return back to Argentina? Besides using that surprise $75 visa (it's good for 10 years, you know).

Is it Florida Avenida? A pedestrian street at least two kilometers long with the highest concentration of leather shops (they eat A LOT of beef here), Peruvian trash art (sailboats in broken light bulbs come to mind), Burger Kings (Yippee... I mean boo), and a gazillion men whispering "cambio" every five seconds (I can hear their inkjet printers pumping out those 100 peso bills by the pound).

Is it Ugi's Pizza? A $3 medium pizza with fresh mozzarella, made in front of you, in a store front that looks more like it should be selling boxing tickets rather than pizza by the slice. But, oh man, does he whip up a good pizza! I can almost imagine resurrecting my old pizza shop back up again to mimic my Ugi friend (just a joke Cindy – please, put the fry pan down!).

Maybe it's the family market store you find about every 50 yards? Five items of the most popular food, toiletries, sweets, and milk in a bag on the 15 shelves they have. "If only I could pry the owner away from the TV he's watching, I could buy my Kinder Sorpresa Egg and be outta here. Oh wait, it's the Boca versus River soccer game... *Can you scoot over a bit? I'll buy the Fanta!*"

Or possibly, it's the panaderias? "Give me six rolls of bread, una docena of Alfajores, three empanadas de carne and de pollo and de jamon y queso. Ah shoot, give me six of everything. I'll be back in the morning for the pastries (medialunas... mas por favor!)."

Maybe it's the country's pride, displayed everywhere by the Argentinian flag.

Maybe the natural wonders we missed – Patagonia, Mar Del Plata, Mendoza's Andes, and those darn cute penguins somewhere down south.

Realistically, it is probably a bit of everything that makes me excited to go back. It's Argentina magic... a country where craziness coexists with order... where culture and tradition is mixed with international flare... and where a family of five comfortably called Buenos Aires home for a month... and loved it!

# Chapter 3:  Costa Rica:

# Son of a Beach... Now That's What I Call a Beach!

Humorous Insights

# For Once in My Life, I May Actually be a Genius

I don't profess to be a genius, though I secretly want to be seen as one. Who doesn't, right? And for some reason, every time I think I am on top of the mountain – at that point of perfect superiority – someone either pushes me off of the peak or points out that what I'm currently standing on is actually a stepping-stone to the Himalayan climb I truly face. Really sucks!

But everyone has moments when they truly are a genius... even if it only lasts a second or two.

Leaving Argentina was tough. I was feeling smart for going – dumb for picking the winter – but still intelligent enough to have picked it as a place to visit. I was excited for the prospects of Costa Rica making me the next Einstein in my family's eyes.

When we arrived in San Jose, I thought that visiting the capital would be an adventure and we would learn a lot about the country. Well, we sure learned a lot fast, such as, in the words of our Taxi driver, "San Jose is feo (ugly)... you need to go to the beach. This place is no good."

Okay, one man's opinion. Some people just don't like the city, right?

I asked the rental car agent what there was to see in San Jose. "Nothing, there is nothing. Don't go downtown, don't go walking around, it's best to drive out of here. Go to the beach!"

Wow, I had either found the Anti-San Jose Club or we might have been on to something bigger. So we determined to do what any sensible person would do — we went downtown. If it was out of spite or pure curiosity, I couldn't tell you.

San Jose, San Jose, San Jose. What can be said about San Jose. It was an adventure. More shanty houses and McDonald's than there are taxis (note: there are a lot of taxis. In fact, there are more taxis than there are... more than... I don't know... let's just say a lot!). Congestion, traffic, confusion, and — I sound like I just joined the Anti-San Jose Club.

However, we luckily did go downtown because we ended up at the Museo De Oro (Museum Of Gold), an amazing museum that houses one of the best and most complete collections of Pre-Colombian gold structures and art on the planet. You walk around in an underground vault (think Superman's fortress of solitude with armed guards everywhere). Once inside, you are free to walk around the exhibit and examine these small, intricately designed gold pieces. It was really cool and the cameras never saw me take that solid gold statue. Boy was that heavy!

Our wandering was cut short as we got rained out (don't call us sissies, Costa Rica rain can drown a grown man standing up). We were only able to drive around a bit the next day due to the rain also. I was eating crow right then. Cindy was giving me that look of: "and why did you drag the kids and me here?" I was feeling like I had just flunked out of kindergarten. I was nowhere near genius status.

So, we were happy to be on to Puerto Viejo, on the Caribbean South side of Costa Rica. The drive took a few hours, in which we went through a rainforest (and amazingly it was raining), a few miles of pineapple fields, then a few miles of banana fields, a few more miles of pineapple fields, there were Pipa (fruit and food) stands everywhere (*Pipa Ellis* had a ton of people eating there – Ellis must whip up a mean bowl of beans and rice), and finally through Limon with its semi-truck convention. A half hour jaunt south from Limon led us to Puerto Viejo – our home for the next three weeks.

So, you might ask... How was it?

I found myself standing on a deserted beach – with no one else visible for as far as I could see. And I mean miles. It was just me, my wife and three daughters splashing around on a beach next to the Caribbean Sea, the jungle stretching into the sand and the sun tucking into the pillow clouds. At that moment, for that brief second... I was a genius!

This is Costa Rica! Pura Vida!

# Scuba Diving In Puerto Viejo

Scuba diving was something I had wanted to do forever. There is something about floating along with fish 20-feet below the surface and not worrying about swimming and gasping for air that fascinates me. So, becoming a certified open water diver was one of my life goals for a few years.

Before our trip, I unsuccessfully tried to get a group of friends and family to do scuba diving with me. It didn't work out. Something about no one wanting to open water dive in Lake Mead (the pool of water by Las Vegas famous for its floating tumbleweeds: "Yeppee! A floating tumbleweed... Ouch, it's a floating tumbleweed!").

Let's just make things clear about my nautical talent. I'm an okay swimmer but don't start drowning next to me – you may sink to the ocean bottom. Learning to swim in Cub Scouts with a life-jacket isn't one of my proudest moments.

So, here we were in Costa Rica, next to a beach and the best coral in the country (it is not the US Virgin Islands, but it was coral). All I needed was a place to get certified. "Oh look, Cindy, I can't believe it... It's a dive shop... what's the possibility of finding a dive shop here?" Gotta love the internet for researching this type of stuff. Once I saw the Reef Runners Dive shop in Puerto Viejo, I was sold on it before I even walked into the office.

Being a semi-laid-back Caribbean town (and a semi-party-til-I-can't-remember-my-own-name town), I wasn't expecting much. But after I talked to my DiveMaster Instructor, I was convinced that this location was perfect for my open dive certification. Why? Personalized instruction and attention. First, it was the off season. Second, Puerto Viejo is somewhat remote. Third, it is a small dive shop (the office is one room about 8 feet by 12 feet - did I mention that the office is the dive shop?). Fourth, it has some of the best coral reefs in Costa Rica. Perfect for a guy who was given the swimming merit badge out of guilt and not ability.

Open water certification involved a book training section and four open water "skill" dives. The book work was interesting and a little repetitive. It was neat to learn about nitrogen intoxication – sounds really funny and really dangerous. It was tiresome being told about 50 times never to hold your breath (though blowing your lungs out on assent is not an experience I would like to try). Once I completed the reading and quizzes, I began my open dives – the meat of the course.

Skill dives encompass learning all of the technical skills you read about. Neutral buoyancy (very important if you don't want to sink to the ocean bottom), emergency controlled assents (don't hold your breath), and skills like replacing your mask in water (salt water up your nose is great for sinus cleansing). If you get this done fast enough, you have time to explore the reef... this is what I am talking about.

What do I think about scuba diving now?

Everyone on the planet should be open water certified. Well, maybe not… if you're a potential hazard to yourself and any aquatic life forms, you can learn to make sand mermaids instead. The appreciation one gains from paddling around a reef is priceless. Seeing trunk fish defend their school, playing with arrow crabs (they are hilarious), spooking a scorpion fish, dodging lion fish, watching anemone wave in the current... OK, you get my point, it is really amazing. It truly is another world and one that few actually explore.

So, next time you get the opportunity to take an open water diving certification class, and you are debating whether you should do it or not, take it and do it. Don't think twice. Otherwise, you may be limited to sand mermaids – just you sweating in the sand wishing you had taken the dive certification class – and that sounds more pathetic than an 11-year-old swimming with a life-jacket.

# Life on the Beach and Man Versus Everything

When I was working a job before Costa Rica - yes, I held a serious full time job before Costa Rica - I used to fantasize about living on the beach, watching the waves roll along and eating coconuts and bananas. One day, that would be me... I would be the one relaxing. No worries, no deadlines, no phone, no nothing. Now that sounded like pure paradise!

So, for three full, wonderful weeks we lived on the beach. We played in the surf, ate enough bananas to make a monkey puke, listened to the waves crash every day, swung in the hammock while reading a good book, listened to the tropic birds sing us songs... It was blissful.

But, the balance of the Universe has to be maintained. There must be something to counterbalance all this positive Chi, right? I mean, for every action, there has to be a reciprocal reaction. For every positive up tick, there has to be a negative down tick (now for you thermodynamic freaks out there, thinking entropy is constantly creating chaos, stick your head in a bucket for five minutes and don't talk to me right now). There has to be something to balance all this goodness I have been inhaling, right?

Right!

It's called Man versus Everything!

Before you go nuts on me here and think I'm a complete anti-nature loon, drinking too many over-ripe coconuts, hear me out.

Imagine this. You are swinging peacefully in a hammock, not bothering anyone, listening to the ocean in pure bliss, and without warning a snake falls out of the bush next to you. "Holy Crap! There are like six million poisonous types of snakes in Costa Rica... that sucker could have bit my face right off!"

Okay, it was a vine snake. Small. Maybe even an infant. Couldn't have hurt a flee — maybe a small rodent, but definitely not me — at least, not all at once.

Now imagine this. You are in the rainforest, watching poison dart frogs chirp. "Wait, are those toucans that just flew by? This is amazing! This is one of the coolest... OUCH!" You just so happened to be standing in the war zone of a bunch of army ants. You run for your life, knowing that you can outrun 90% of all living rainforest creatures (heaven help us with those 10% you can't outrun). Later, upon looking at the gazillion bites you have on your ankles, you notice that you were bitten by something else... all over your arms, neck, legs. They even ate through your socks! These guys are ruthless!

Alright, the ants didn't bite me. They were dang close though. I swear they were eyeballing me too. The arm, neck and leg bites weren't from mosquitoes but from what Cindy calls "No-See-Ems" since you really don't see them until you kill them and as they are biting you, of course, not before. The outcome is a few bites, a couple days of itching like a madman, but nothing long-term.

How about this? You are playing at the beach, having a great time finding sand dollars and seashells. You and your daughter are thoroughly enjoying looking at the small tropical fish in the coral close by. Your daughter reaches down into the sand for that perfect shell, then "OUCH! Daddy, something just bit me!" A medium sized sand crab scurries off for shelter. Starting to cry, your daughter asks you amidst endless tears, "Daddy, I didn't do anything to him. I didn't want to hurt him! Why did it pinch me? WHY Daddy?"

The reality? It was a small cut. She was traumatized for a few minutes but if you were the crab about to be squashed by a giant, what would you do? She was over it and chasing crabs in a half hour.

Conclusion: The Universe has perfect harmony. There can't be pleasure without pain. There can't be Yin without Yang. With every positive, there is a negative.

Did I fully explain the magnitude of the negative? Let me put it in this way:

Getting eaten by Nature is a small price to pay for having a hammock overlooking the Caribbean Sea for weeks, not being behind that office desk from hell, no worries, no bosses... AAHHH! The Universe is my friend!

Ouch! Dang "No-See-Ems."

# Why There are No Stupid People in Costa Rica

They say New Zealand is the capital of high adventure and the thrill industry. Up to this point, Costa Rica had to have the most ziplines, white water rafting, hiking, jungle adventures than anywhere I had been.

So, you're asking, why do I think that there are no stupid people in Costa Rica? Let me explain with a few stories.

Example One:

We went to La Fortuna, Costa Rica. This town ("The Fortune") is located right next to the most active volcano in the country, Arenal. This volcano happens to also be one of the ten most active volcanos in the Ring Of Fire. Now that is something to be proud of, right? No one has been killed since 1968, when a whole town that was built on the volcano's side got blown up. The volcano only spits out a few rocks now and then, a hungry grumble every few hours, a puff of smoke once a day or so, just to remind the natives who's boss. So let's build a big city and develop tons of activities for the tourists to come to. Sounds like a good idea, right?

So, we went to Ecoglide, a zipline company right on the side of the volcano. We got suited up and drove another half-mile up the mountain. One of our guides, Hanzel (no, I'm not making this up. He said his name was Hanzel and it was scribbled on his badge – though this could be corporate hazing – I never got a feel for labor laws in Costa Rica), told us that from the first platform, we could hike right up to the volcano peak.

Curious, I asked, "Can you hike the volcano?" I was surprised to hear someone actually purposing going up to the peak.

"Sure," Hanzel quickly replied. "You could... you would die, but you could. Let me explain. You hike in the jungle, a snake will probably bite you and you die. If not, the ground is very wet, you probably would slip and fall down the mountain and die. If those don't kill you, the volcano will."

So, you can climb it, technically, but you would be dead. Okay, sounds reasonable.

Example Two:

We went to Tortuguero, on the northeast coast of Costa Rica. To get there, you must drive through a million banana and pineapple farms and eventually take a small riverboat through alligator-infested waters. Sidenote: the riverboat ride was way better than the Disneyland Jungle Cruise. I asked if anyone swam in the water. "Oh no, you get killed." Interesting. So I asked if they prefer to swim in the ocean. "Oh no, the riptides will grab you and kill you. We prefer to swim in the river." Yes, this is the same alligator-infested river. Go figure.

Example Three:

The western side of Costa Rica had torrential rains for two solid months before we arrived in the country. This unusual quantity of rain caused massive mudslides, flooding, and parts of roads to disappear. We luckily spent most of our time in the Limon providence and it was in a dry season... for a month (weird but true). So, as great American tourists with children, the prudent thing to do was to drive through these mudslides and see the west coast.

Did I ever tell you about Cindy and the three girls all throwing up as we drove through the mountain roads of Puerto Rico? Well, we almost had the sequel.

These roads are everywhere – up and down and whipping right to left – everywhere. We only had to stop once so that the girls (including Cindy) could feel solid ground for 15 minutes and recuperate. During this drive, we saw roads that hugged several hundred feet drops, bridges that accommodated half a mid-sized car, goats that seem to own the road, and enough coffee plants to wire up a college freshman class for years.

At one point, we waited an hour to cross over a temporary bridge that was constructed after a mudslide wiped out the road. I have no idea where they pulled this bridge from but it reminded me of the construction sets I played with as a kid. Semis rolled over them, buses crossed them and we crossed it. I think Cindy had her eyes closed, mumbling something like "Oh, please spare us... I've been really nice to Richard lately... that has to count for something." Just joking, she said "Richard... stop taking pictures and drive the dumb car!" Okay, really, she said nothing. I don't even think she was breathing during the whole crossing but that isn't as funny as her praying for salvation or getting mad at me.

These roads are Costa Rica's main roads, too – that's why semis were on them, big garbage trucks – everyone who didn't have something better to do was on this road. And Costa Rican drivers are all in a race. They get behind the wheel and the demon comes out. Zoom! Screech! Zoom! There might be a few Honk! Honk!'s in there too.

Now, again... why do I think there are no stupid people in Costa Rica?

Simple, because the stupid people are all dead! That's why. If the jungle hasn't eaten them 'cause they thought a quick run through the bush would be refreshing, a volcano hasn't crushed them while they were conquering the next hill, some nutty animal didn't snap them in half while swimming in their neighbor's pool, or finally, they didn't run off the road like Thelma and Louise or the Dukes of Hazard, then they are certified intelligent. A stupid person can't possibly survive the elements of Costa Rica.

So now you wonder how I survived? Yeah, I can hear you thinking that.

Well, that is just a really stupid question. Why don't you just come to Costa Rica so I can show you around? Hehe.

# Chapter 4:  Samoa:

## He Doesn't Look Silly in Flip Flops Because He's a 500-Pound Slab of Muscle!

Humorous Insights

# Land of The Flip-Flopping Muscle Gang

Back in Argentina, we met a girl from New Zealand during our empanada cooking class. As we chopped vegetables, we exchanged travel stories. She and her friend were on a three-month backpacking trip around South America (a brilliant idea... I'll pencil that in for 2020). After a while, she asked about our trip. When she found out we were going to Samoa, she brightened up and said, "Fantastic. You'll love it! How long are you staying?" When I told her a month, her face changed from delight to "Are you serious?" After a little bit more chatting, she basically informed us that we would have a weeks' worth of stuff to do and then be bored for the remaining time.

After almost a week in Samoa, I would have to say, she was absolutely right! Empanadas are one of the best foods in Argentina. About Samoa, she must have been on some other island.

...or maybe, she just didn't understand Samoa.

Some people will come to Upolu, the populated island, and see a few sites and leave. Maybe that's all they wanted. Well, the tragedy of this plan is you miss the Samoan culture, which in my opinion, turned out to be the best part of being on the island. As always, let me explain.

First, if you walk around Apia (Samoa's capitol) during the day, you see a busy town. Now it's not a big city by US standards, but it would be a good-sized town. People everywhere. People everywhere in lavalavas (a wraparound cloth for covering your lower body). Now I am careful here not to call it a wrap-around skirt... for two reasons: One, men wear these lavalavas and men don't wear skirts. Two, Samoan men wear these lavalavas, and I don't know about you but I would not be the first one asking a Samoan man why he was wearing a skirt.

Why is this dangerous? Let me explain.

Samoan men. Most have more muscles in their forearm than I have in my entire body. I've tried to figure out why the men are genetically huge like this. It can't be from banana, papaya, or taro. Coconuts wouldn't do it either. Fish? No way. So, naturally, I figure it has to do with volcanos. Let me explain.

"Hey Jimmy" - Jimmy happens to be the skinny kid in the village - "You can be a member of the muscle kid gang if you can jump across the volcano crater." Jimmy thinks about this for a second, "Nah. That doesn't sound like a good idea. How about measuring the caloric in-take from bananas, papayas, and taros?" At this, the big muscular kids giggle and grab the skinny kid and throw him into the volcano anyway. The village thinks this is hilarious. They gather up all the skinny kids, and as a sport, throw them one by one into the volcano. This sport becomes a national pastime until they run out of non-muscular kids. This has to be why they attacked Tonga and Fiji for so many years – they needed more skinny kids to chuck into volcanos. They then ran out of skinny kids in Polynesia and it was a big problem... until recently. Let me explain.

As we walked around Apia, everyone was really nice to me. I walked down the road and people smiled at me and said "Hello" or "Talofa" or simply smiled and waved. I would drive down the road and I would get people waving at me also. People were super nice there. I mean, the whole population has this unbelievable friendliness about them. It might be the nicest place I've ever been. This scared me.

Why did this scare me? Let me explain.

I'm skinny. I've never been asked to be a member of a muscle-kid gang, nor would I want to be. As I looked around Apia, I really didn't see anyone who isn't a member of the muscle kid gang. The five-year olds, for crying-out-loud, were walking around with several large rocks in their hands. OK, I'm exaggerating... they were only walking around with one massive rock in their hands. I didn't see anyone who couldn't smash through a brick wall. As they smiled at me, I couldn't help but wonder if the whole place was thinking "We finally have a skinny kid. Let's take him to Mount Matavanu! We'll tell him it has pretty lights."

So, during this story, you learned some interesting facts about Samoans... they wear lavalavas, the national footwear is flip-flops, Samoan men rip down trees with their bare hands, they smile and wave at everyone, and life is simple... and did I mention they love ice cream (my kind of place).

Really though, discovering a new culture is amazing and entertaining. Your brain starts imagining what the people eat, what the local traditions are, and what activities they do for fun. The whole thing is an adventure, even going to the grocery store and counting how many different types of SPAM there are (bacon-flavored?).

Sure, Samoa had touristy stuff to go and do, and I wanted to do them... but the meat and potatoes (or Pig and Taros) of coming to Samoa was getting to know the Polynesian way of life. Samoans call it "Fa'a Samoa," or the Samoan Way. The laid-back, happy way of life they have there made me happy. It made me want to stay more than a month because you know they were on to something more important. Things like family, friends, and good food. This is culture.

Though, I can't help second guessing that invitation I was given. Being invited to be the guest of honor at a "Barbecue" sounded suspiciously like: "Let's go throw the skinny guy into the volcano." Hey, if it was true, it would at least have been a cultural adventure... and maybe they would have had ice cream.

# Random Thoughts about Samoa

Two weeks into our visit in Samoa and another three weeks to go, I felt like I was starting to get a good understanding of Samoa. Here are a few thoughts, ideas, opinions, theories, and pure speculations. Let it be known, I have put a lot of thought into these thoughts, ideas, opinions, theories, and pure speculations, so you can take it for "Gospel Truth!"

## The Speed Limit is Set by How Fast a Pig Can Run across the Road and Not Get Squashed.

Pigs and chickens are a staple of any quality Samoan village. They roam freely and to my knowledge, have full authority to eat, sleep, and "you know what" anywhere they want. Since they are a food supply, they aren't allowed to be hurt by rambunctious, speed-crazed, motor vehicles.

We put this speed-limit-to-pig-speed theory to the test in Savaii, the big island to the Samoans. Side note: Our taxi driver was born to drive cars. Not only did he go twice the speed limit, he could honk the horn, flash his lights, talk on the phone, and wave at his friends simultaneously; of course, there was no one else on the road. Made it all seem OK. Anyway, a piglet decided to cross the road (mental note to save this pig joke for later) as we were rocketing down the road. Ieti (pronounced "It" - well, that's what I heard) slammed on the brakes, decelerating until he reached the speed limit, thereby narrowly missing the squealing piglet.

Proof that pigs are saved by the pork-loving Samoan Parliament and their friendly traffic laws.

## If There Happens to be Something a Tourist Would Pay to See, Some Samoan Village Has it and Will Charge You for it.

Take the family waterfall tour we took by car as an example of Samoan capitalism. We drove around Upolu in a large circle to see these South Pacific waterfall wonders. Each place had a fale (grass hut) strategically located in front of these natural marvels, making it impossible to sneak by without paying their fee. These villages must have thought a thousand years ago that someday it would pay off to locate close to a waterfall; they just had to live with the corresponding 500 foot cliff next to that waterfall and deal with their kids falling off a couple times a month.

Let's be clear here to what I'm complaining about: it was not a lot of money, it was having to pay for a two minute glance. These pay stations just didn't make me happy inside. Call it cost versus benefit. Call it being swindled by a Samoan (It seemed to happen to me a lot. They just started smiling at me and I was toast. I can't negotiate with someone smiling bigger than I am smiling). Call it fantastic to not do anything and get paid by Tala-toting tourists. I don't know, call it something... of course, it did make me laugh inside to see how good they played this game. Maybe I should start my own Samoan-village tourist trap in Houston. That is not a bad idea. Time to swindle. Wait, we don't have waterfalls.

## There is a Samoan book out there named 1001 Ways to Use Palm Fronds.

I haven't seen this book personally, but it's out there. The Martha Stewart of Samoa wrote this book many generations ago and it was a solid hit. Such a hit, that everyone makes woven baskets the same, fales the same, tapa mats the same... everything the same. This author discovered palm leaf necklaces, palm leaf book covers, and the palm leaf skirt (not that popular in today's society... something to do with modesty in windy weather). Whoever this Samoan was, he or she had to have a great life... Laying around, watching the world go by, charging Tala-toting Samoans for their copy of the book, smiling really big to confuse the negotiation... perfect serenity.

The best part of all these woven goods is that they're entirely eco-friendly. Children can chew on any fale and not get lead poisoning. If a basket splits open, no worries, throw it in the woods, and go make another one. All materials naturally degrade and aren't products of horrible oil resins. Perfect!

Well, I haven't finished writing up this list, but this was a good start. Time has been good to Samoa. The country still enjoys the slow life along with the small technological advances that others make. So, look forward to that next list... I just have to get another taxi driver to experiment with and find a copy of that darn book. Hope it has pictures 'cause my Samoan is horrific. Tofa!

# Random Thoughts about Samoa #2

Well, here goes a second round of my philosophies regarding Samoa. Remember, these opinions are mine, have not been distorted by crazy National Geographic documentaries, and are completely true... that's why they're my opinions.

## Fruits and Vegetables - Banana and Papaya Are Like Bread and Butter Anywhere Else

Now this might sound strange, but you can't buy bananas in the supermarket. Of course, "supermarket" was a bit of a stretch there in Samoa (but for the context of this bit, just go with me here). You could buy bell peppers and zucchini in a supermarket... sure, you just had to weigh these veggies on a scale and balance it with 24K gold; hand over the gold, take the veggies. Cry as you eat these veggies and discover they taste like plastic. However, bananas and papaya are so common that you can only buy them from local growers in the open market. You buy bananas by the "hand." A hand is about a half rotation around the banana plant... so a good amount. I'm sure Samoans were fascinated by me and my bargaining skills in the market too. Me: "How much for the hand of bananas?" Market Lady: "Two Tala for a hand... they very good bananas." Me: "Great, I'll take it for three Tala." Market Lady (after realizing I'm either dumb or crazy): "You like papaya too?"

# Open Market Souvenirs - Why Pay More for Less?

You see similar souvenirs wherever you go in Samoa... necklaces, miniature fales, lavalavas, and kava bowls. You see them in nice stores, you see them in not so nice stores, and of course, you see them in the open market. Funny thing though – it's the same stuff. There were no major differences that I could tell... so, they had to be from the same supplier.

Buying them in the open market was way more fun than the stores, mainly because there was no price tag. The marketer is hoping to hose you; you are hoping to have your pants when you walk away from the deal or at least most of your dignity. It's all in the negotiation. I found out they all have bosses. Like the mafia. They start out saying it costs this much but because today is the second Tuesday of the month and his favorite pig was born on this day, it's five Tala off. So, you being a seasoned tourist, ask for five Tala less than that. The marketer is so offended that he grabs his Samoan sword and runs after you. Luckily you can run faster in shoes than he can in flip-flops and you escape to your hotel where they call you some word in Samoan that means "Life worth fifteen Tala, thirty Cene."

This of course doesn't happen, but it was what I was worried about. So I would buy two things, get five Tala off this bargain price and we both were smiling. Him because he just hosed a tourist. Me because the hotel could now call me "Life worth hotel room costing 200 Tala a night."

# Internet Cafes are Modern Torture Chambers

This sounds completely random, right? But you haven't had to try to get something done in an internet cafe in Samoa.

First, pay for time: ten Tala for an hour. Five Tala for thirty minutes. And the bargain of all bargains, two Tala for five minutes. The bargain comes with insane reading while you scream and pant. Do you think I'm exaggerating?

Well, what you haven't considered is, as Americans, we slurp off internet time like it is air. Three hours of brainless Facebooking is nothing. People waste time talking about what they just ate (a Spam sandwich), what they are doing right now (picking my nose), and then for those experienced Facebookers... you have the mega time waster of all time, Facebook games (I'm a farmer, yippee!). We are so indifferent at having endless internet time, we play games that make us inclined to tell people how we're doing with our imaginary computer farm. So, when I had a countdown clock staring at me while I tried to check email, do research on New Zealand accommodations, and cyclones in the South Pacific... it became a bit unnerving.

What put me over the edge was that the websites didn't just pop up, they teased me with "Loading" prompts and having to wait extra-long for the page to finally appear. A race against time and Tala.

For example, with five minutes to spare, I received a warning that I was running out of time, the pressure was on to finalize the hotel apartment in Auckland. The screen didn't reload. I refreshed the screen. Wait... Wait... Wait... Refreshed because nothing was happening. Wait... Wait... Wait... Popped up. Enter name, credit card, get ready to press "Submit." Poof. Time was up! I raised my hands into the air. I gritted my teeth in agony. I tilted my head back as I screamed, "Torrrrr-tttttuuuuuuuurrrrreeeee!" Unfortunately, I then had to compose myself enough to pay two Tala for another five minute insanity session.

Well, with a little more than a week and a half left of our Samoan tour of duty, I still wanted to see how good small Samoan children could throw rocks, find out which spam flavor was better – pig or chicken, and why there were more Chinese working in grocery stores than Samoans. I would have found out but I needed to enjoy those internet farm grown bell peppers I grew online in Texas.

# Random Thoughts about Samoa #3

As our Tour Of Samoa came closer to an end, I thought it would only be appropriate to share more random thoughts on how random Samoa is... yes... random.

Random like it is rude to walk around eating ice cream, so a mass quantity of Samoans would huddle in the entrance of the ice cream store licking away at the banana chocolate chip cone (this flavor was good stuff).

Warning: As before, these are my observations and by no means should be taken too seriously, though I would be very insulted if you don't find humor in this as I've worked very hard analyzing these over Ke Ke Pua'a rolls.

Here goes nothing...

## **Samoan's Running Bird**

There's a bird in Samoa... called a Sina Vua. The bird is some weird mix of a Kiwi and a roadrunner. I never saw it fly, only run like a madman across roads, lawns, graves, runways. You name it, it was running over it. I said 'run' as this bird didn't just wander or walk, it was a full out run. It should also be pointed out that this bird had to be part chicken, as it was scared of everything. They wouldn't let you get within a rocks throw of them... and seeing how good little Samoan boys threw rocks, this was probably a good thing.

This bird was my hero. I loved this bird. I don't know why it was so cool to me, but I couldn't get over it. Not only did its disappearing act fascinate me, it made me laugh as it zoomed off like the Looney Tunes' Roadrunner. Maybe that's it; it is Samoa's version of Looney Tunes, and who doesn't love Looney Tunes, right? Beep-Beep-Zip-Tang!

## The Chinese Invasion

Is it just me or does there seem to be a lot of Chinese people in Samoa? Wait, I need to rephrase that as I should never let anyone think it is just me!

Now I love everything Chinese... fortune cookies, chop suey, Buddha... Big fan. I was just surprised at how most of the grocery stores around Apia were run and owned by Chinese, huge government buildings were being constructed solely by Chinese, Chinese restaurants dotted the island...

...though, I believe there is a Chinese restaurant in almost every country on the planet. I can tell you that I have eaten Chinese food in a Chinese restaurant in more than ten countries. Shoot, I even tried to eat Chinese in every country on this trip... Argentina (Check!), Samoa (Check!), USA (Check!)... Costa Rica... darn! Next time.

Side note: Cindy thinks Italy has the best Chinese food in the world. Nothing can be more satisfying than the "Bella Cina" restaurant in Latina, Italy. Was Chinese food in China better than Chinese food in Italy? I am not saying. I will simply restate my favorite Chinese proverb: Confucius say, "Good fortune cookie is bad replacement for lousy Chinese food."

## Palolo Deep

There is a Marine Sanctuary near the wharf in Apia called Palolo Deep. This small recess in the reef has protected the coral and aquatic life for a very long time. Everywhere else around this area, the coral has been destroyed. But here in this small reserve, the coral was splendid. The variety of coral and fish made snorkeling a lot of fun. The girls loved it.

Palolo Deep was also where I met my little friend "Scout." While I was free diving with Sophia, I ended up being the big brother fish for a very small yellow fish with black stripes – one not bigger than an inch, two inches max. Sophia named him Scout because she thought he was quite adventurous. If I am correct, I picked up this little guy while I dove down, it spotted me, thought it was a good idea to follow me back up to the surface, and proceeded to swim under my belly for a half hour... ending up at the shore where I got out. I can imagine the complete dread from his little brain as his big fish friend popped out of the water and deserted him. "Where did he go? He was here, now he's not here. I don't know where I am... hey, that means I'm lost. AUGH!"

It was also a little disheartening to be seen as large enough for small fish to follow. Sob! I instead will continue to try focusing on how he tickled my stomach as I splashed along. That's a happy thought.

Scout, wherever you may be, don't end up following those freight liners; you'll end up in China, being caught by a fisherman, sold to a restaurant, stuffed into a spring roll or something tasty, and I'm bound to eat you in another one of those Chinese restaurants.

...and that would really suck.

# Chapter 5: New Zealand:

# How a Kiwi Can Eat a Kiwi That Just Ate a Kiwi

Humorous Insights

©2015

# Campervanland New Zealand

Auckland, New Zealand is one of the cleanest, prettiest, most modern cities I've ever been to. It was also expensive – before you disagree with me or trash talk about me, remember we had just come from Samoa where I could buy a chilled coconut to drink for about 40 cents. And then the exchange rate is like 1.25 New Zealand dollars to 1 US dollar. So, when you see something like a Twix candy bar in a convenience store for NZD$3, you choke a little.

But as the Kiwis say, "no worries, mate", because we were living the dream on the South Island. Who would complain about a pricey candy bar when there are penguins to find? How expensive are penguins again? Gulp!

What was it like? Well, the Aucklanders (I'm guessing they're called this – if not, I'm using my creative license as an engineer here) would all ask if we had been to the South Island yet. Upon hearing we're going, they beamed up proudly and say "good 'aye... yus kiwi tenk duh Sawth Ayeland es mauvelus!" Well... that's what my ears heard anyway, it's the whole accent thing. Though I was told that my American accent didn't have a good Texas twang to it. Long story short, the Kiwis think the South Island is the bomb. And I have to agree.

First, we flew into Christchurch. I should have done a social experiment on how religious the general population was –

demented Richard fun – but with a city name like Christchurch, you have to wonder how many atheists live there. We left the airport and went straight into a campervan. New Zealand uses "campervan" for motorhome or RV. And they use "holiday park" for RV park or campsite. I only wish I could have figured this out while I was in the planning phase... I would have worked a few things out better.

You can't simply park your campervan wherever you like either. This is a major taboo. There are stories of rambunctious campervan folk parking where they shouldn't and being eaten by blue penguins – which are the world's smallest penguins, but they are New Zealand penguins and can rugby slam anything 20 times its size, just ask the Australian penguins. And you ask, "are there Australian penguins?" I don't know, but if there's not, they probably became extinct because they improperly parked their campervan somewhere on the South Island of New Zealand.

Campervanning was tons of fun though. You haul all your crap with you – no major packing up every morning, you simply rearrange your dump so that you can at least drive away and you're set. You can cook your own meals, do school work, sleep in them, shoot, I can even take a $#!* in it. If it told jokes, I would sell the house in Texas, buy one, and live forever in it. Just don't tell Cindy. She has suspected this scheme and has begun developing a counter-attack to it. Clever woman.

Back to New Zealand though. This population loves the campervan. There are more accommodations for tents and campervans than anything else I've seen. No need to plan too far ahead either – just drive in a general direction and find out what there is to see there. This worked great for us. The adventure of not knowing what you will do tomorrow was quite rewarding. No stress, no problems, no worries. And there was so much nature to be seen in New Zealand, it was almost incomprehensible.

Don't believe me? Here's a sample of 3 days' worth of campervanning.

Huge stone spheres laying on a beach. No, it's not cruise ship waste from Mexico – yuck, that's really a gross thought. These boulders were formed over thousands of years of accumulating matter on them. They eventually got larger and larger until they were big enough for tourists to stand on them and take lots of photos. Super cool, right?

How about seeing the nine-foot long wingspans of the royal albatross. The albatross look like small airplanes zooming around. I actually gasped in surprise when one zipped by me unsuspectingly. For me to gasp, you have to seriously impress me (well, maybe impress is too strong, let's say shock) or hurt me in ways only my four foot daughter could do when she runs really fast and hugs me too quickly (run, hug, crack, moan, bend over, gasp, cry... fall to the ground... you men out there understand gasping when the phrase "head butt to the groin" is said). Anyway, these albatross are really big and impressive – I mean shocking.

And that doesn't even mention the coastal cruising, dolphin watching, fiord crossing, glacier gazing, mountain gawking, Maori admiring, and tourist shop stuff buying. Holy Kiwi, was that price in New Zealand dollars or US dollars?

At this point, we had no idea what we would be doing, but we knew we were going to have a good time doing it. So as a new campervan adventurer, my new motto became: "Kids, move the crap to the left side, I'm driving us outta here."

# Come to New Zealand and Scream Like a Little Girl

Remember a few stories ago when I said that there are some crazy Costa Rican adventure junkies out there? Well, they looked like pansies next to a New Zealander. Don't believe me? Well, I wouldn't expect you to. A gentleman at a ticket counter put it best, "This is the South Island, mate, anything that could happen here does!"

We found that there are more ways to scare the crap out of you in New Zealand than anywhere else in the world. Now this is a broad statement and I'm sure there are those out there that will disagree, but do their extreme sports rate the level of participant terror by how many undershorts are pooed in? For once, I'm not exaggerating. For example, "Five Crapped-Out Undershorts out of Five Possible Crapped-Out Undershorts!" was on an ad in a travel center. I think one crapped-out undershorts is one too many... but not in New Zealand. If they can scare you into an uncontrolled fit of little girl screams, the New Zealanders are only half satisfied. Another advertisement published a tourist's comment as follows, "It was so scary my $#@* was scared $#@*-less!" Now that is an adrenaline junkie at the extreme.

So what crazy adventures can you do in New Zealand to blow holes in your pants?

First, you need to fly into Christchurch and head West to Queenstown, a town that reminds me of Lake Tahoe only a lot more New Zealanders and much more screaming.

Speaking of screaming... Upon arriving in Queenstown, my daughters asked, "Why is it called Queenstown?" The conversation went as follows:

> "Back about 100 years ago there was a guy named... wow, did you see that possum? It just ran in front of that car! Ooooh... gross! Oh, please don't cry. Possums are nasty rodents. They're not native to New Zealand anyway. Man, the animals aren't even safe."

Once you are in Queenstown, you can ride super-fast jetboats where you zoom up rivers and over lakes like a volcano was erupting immediately behind you. "We're going to die! AGHH! What, oh... he was only driving like that to terrorize us? Oh, that's why we paid $65 each... makes sense. Margaret, you hearing this? Margaret? Margaret? Where is Margaret?" In fact, while listening one day to the radio, we heard that a group of tourists were sent to the hospital with whiplash from an over aggressive boat driver. I wonder if that was a two or three crapped out undershorts award?

Or, you can paraglide from the mountain down to the town. See how close you can brush up to 150 foot trees... "Weeeee! Ouch! Weeee! Hey, I think I'm bleeding." And then spiral uncontrollably to a landing site somewhere on the other side of Queenstown's buildings. "AGGGHHH... oh, we're on the ground... hehehe... that was so *barf* fun! Medic!"

How about bungy jumping (bungee – for us Americans) at the birth place of bungy jumping, the original AJ Hacket Bungy just outside of Queenstown on the Wakarau Bridge. Yep, for under $200 you can jump off a wooden bridge that, as Cindy says, "is a perfectly good bridge... so why would you jump off of it?" Well, it's simple. Take the Japanese lady that watched her son jump and then jumped herself as an example. Translating her exact Japanese words into English, as she jumped she gave these words of advice, "GASP! AGGGHHH!" Then her head was submerged under water and I didn't get the rest of her wisdom.

Amazement. That was what I was in. Pure amazement at how we humans have that desire to test fate. Test death's grasp by jumping out of airplanes, canyon swinging, or river surfing (actually, this looked perfectly safe next to everything else). We are so excited to do all of these hazardous activities and call them fun that we are willing to pay lots of money to do them. We are even willing to sign forms that release all fault of death, decapitation or bodily harm to participate in these activities. And the main question is, "What makes us comfortable to do these crazy deeds?"

Engineers.

Yep, we all trust that some engineer worked out the numbers, designed the ropes and safety equipment with lots of tolerances to overcome any possible mishap, and gave the thumbs up to let the masses crap their pants... or is that undershorts?

And as an engineer, I am sorely disappointed that I didn't participate in any of it. Hey, don't make fun of me. I saved money on undershorts.

Why didn't I risk my life doing typical New Zealand adventure? I put all blame on the sprained ankle I got just before leaving Samoa. It was just barely getting to the point where I could walk and not look like Igor when we entered Queenstown.

Dumb excuse? Nonsense! A bum ankle is very incapacitating and makes simple life difficult. OK, I'm lying. It's all Man Machismo. Could you imagine my daughters' image of their father crying and screaming like a little girl while being pushed off the bungy platform? I would never live that down.

And worse, there was no escape from the humiliation. I had another seven months with the family, full time, 24/7. The teasing would be relentless and I just couldn't take that. I will just have to wonder which extreme sport would have made me lose control over my bowels.

As they say, "Have to leave something for next time, right?" And the best part, I'll probably be in Depend Undergarments anyway by then.

# New Zealand - Land Of The Warning Signs

It's not always easy to drive in "The Nation Under The World."

First, you have to drive on the left side of the road. This appears pretty easy at first — especially with cars coming directly towards you in the right lane. Being a Kiwi driver falls to pieces once you approach a roundabout. These road circles are strictly yield-based and not for the timid. "Do you look right then left or just right... Is this guy turning or continuing? Crap, I'm going for it." HONK! "Oops... sorry. I was weak and looked left."

It's not just the left hand driving that was strange. The right sided steering setup blew my mind, which was why I found myself activating the windshield wipers instead of the turn signal. The signage also completely lost me. There were tons of big yellow and orange caution signs that could have meant anything.

Never fear, sign translator is here! Cue Indiana Jones theme music. Yep, I am a certified sign reader and put meaning to simple signs you find while wandering around the planet. With my intuitive insight, you will never go wrong. And if you do, "No hablo Ingles!" works wonders with police officers.

So, before you travel to New Zealand, you must memorize and be aware of the following signs.

**Racing Ahead.** This nice, big sign usually means "Slippery When Wet," however my keen eye and mental interpretation assures me that it really means "Watch Out! New Zealander Race Car Driving Ahead." Now you might think I am a mild driver. However, as my wife can attest, I would rather have a jet engine than a V8 (the motor, not the drink). The typical New Zealander makes me look like a pimple faced teenager in Driver's Ed. New Zealanders have no fear. Dirt road, thousand foot cliff, no worries, pass on the right, honk their thanks, make dust for me to eat. Amazing.

**Beware of sheep**. These mammals are everywhere. I didn't have any idea why there are so many. But they are out there. Staring, watching, eating, and chewing... did you know that that's about all a sheep does? Stare, eat, and chew. I didn't even see one lay down the entire time I was in the country. Sheep are in constant chewing and staring motion. If one is not grinding on some grass, it has to be dead. Honest. Sheep look like they are scheming too. That's why they are staring all the time. Thinking of a plan to take over the place. First, New Zealand then the... can sheep swim?

**Watch out for penguins.** Can you believe there is a sign in New Zealand to watch out for penguins? I'm sorry, but this is too cool. A penguin caution sign. Which makes me wonder, if someone didn't heed a penguin yield sign and ran a little guy over, is that like the worst thing someone could ever do? Riots would unfold, torches, signs wanting your head on a stick, yelling, crying, police with those plastic shields (hehe, plastic shields... what are they thinking? Oh they're not, 'cause they brought a fire hose too).

**Ducks.** You may think, "Ducks? Like little ducks are going to need a caution sign?" My friend, the sign had nothing to do with protecting the ducks, it was about protecting people. I was assaulted by a duck in the city of Picton that wanted my sandwich. It's beady eyes glared at me for minutes. Darn thing wasn't even scared of my size 13 foot. I tried to intimidate it. No good. I tried to run after it in an attempt to scare it away. Instead, it just did a circle on me. Then it tried to fly and grab my sandwich right out of my hand. If it wasn't for my ninja reflexes, my sandwich would have been digesting in that pirate duck's belly. Beware of the beady eyes!

**Exclamation point**. Now, if a big, yellow caution sign isn't enough to get your point across, try it with a huge exclamation point. It's like yelling in email with all caps. SLOW DOWN YOU MORON! See, it works. Here though, it's EXCLAMATION POINT... we kinda put a rumble strip down... if you could, uh, kinda, look out for that... meaning, uh, if you hear something weird, it's not your rundown rental car losing its tires... it's the rumble strip we put up... so EXCLAMATION POINT!!!

See how much you learned today. Aren't you glad you listened to me for once?

Well fine then, be that way, I won't tell you what this sign means...

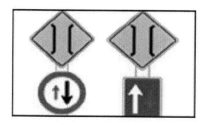

And good luck with parallel parking on the opposite side of the street.

# New Zealand - a World to Itself

I can't think about New Zealand without giving some mention to a few New Zealand favorites – Kiwis, glaciers, Hobbits, and glowworms.

## The Hunt for Kiwi.

There used to be millions of Kiwi birds. I could imagine them grazing the abundant slopes much like the sheep graze now, except, this would have to be at night because kiwi are nocturnal and they eat bugs and worms in the dirt. And they are earthy colors and would be hard to see unlike the white sheep. So, imagine seeing a peaceful hillside with nothing you can see on it. Anyway, there used to be lots of them and now there are like 700,000 and declining. With such few in number, it doesn't surprise me that we didn't see one until the last week of us being in New Zealand. That's when we went to a Maori cultural center and saw a geyser.

Wooo. That's confusing but it's exactly how it happened.

In the city of Rotorua, there are several Maori villages and a cultural center called Te Puia. This center is in the middle of a good sized caldera. For you non-volcanologists, this is an area of high thermal activity in the form of geysers and hot pots. Think Yellowstone and Old Faithful and you are there. We learned that the Maori, in their utmost wisdom, used the hot springs and geysers for basic domestic needs: cooking, cleaning, heating, humor.

Imagine a tribe of Maori that just caught a slew of fish. The fire that was going to be used to cook lunch just got put out by a passing rain storm. One young warrior, hungry for some good fish, says, "Hey, why don't we dunk these whoppers in the steambath?" About 20 head slaps occur simultaneously to signify the years wasted starting fires next to these hot pots. The young warrior is promoted to "Smart Guy" and for centuries these Maori cook all their meals "Al Fondue."

So, as tourists came to see the hot springs and Maori culture, they naturally asked what a Kiwi tastes like. This seriously offended the Maori and the tourists were killed and their brains eaten. Though, from here the Maori began thinking, "yes, a kiwi house would be a perfect tourist attraction" and they went out and made the house that day.

I loved Te Puia simply because it rolled up three of the main themes of New Zealand: the Maori, the high tectonic activity, and kiwi. If you have only a few days in New Zealand, the Te Puia center could save you days of wandering.

## Glowworms that Glow

You have to love bugs that glow in the dark. These insects are every kid's dream. Imagine worms that look like clear gummy worms and have bums that glow a beautiful blue when they are hungry. Hehe, when was the last time you said worm, bum, beautiful, and hungry in the same sentence? Sorry, just the kid inside bubbling up.

One thing that most tourist places won't tell you is that these glowworms are everywhere. Unfortunately, to see them in large clusters, you really need to go to a cave or den where they get enough moisture, protection, and food. There are several popular places to see them: the Waitomo Caves on the North Island (expensive but awesome), the Glowworm Caves in Te Anau on the South Island (expensive but awesome), and Hotikita (where you walk across the street and see them for free! Crazy Awesome!).

Nothing bites me more than paying a butt load of money to see really cool bugs when I can see them for free five days later.

Anyway, whether you see them for free or pay the big bucks, it is worth the trouble. Beautiful, hungry, glowy bugs! Still makes me giggle.

## Glaciers Make Me Happy

There are two main glaciers that folks can visit easily in New Zealand. One is Fox Glacier, the other is Franz Josef Glacier. Both are really cool and both can be walked up to without a guide so don't be fooled into a tour if all you want to do is a quick hike and take pictures.

If you want more of an adventure, take the half day hike and then you can walk on the ice. We are saving this activity for when Cindy and I go back alone – that way we won't have the guilt of a child lost in some massive gap in the ice cracks of gigantic glaciers. Always have to save a bit for next time. The walking on ice bit, that is... not losing a kid to a natural disaster.

## Penguins are Cooler than Blue Glowing Worms

Seeing penguins in the wild can be a coma inducing experience. After waiting for an hour without seeing a penguin and just when you are about to give up, a penguin jumps out of the water from nowhere. Watching a penguin climb rocks has to be one of the funniest things ever to watch. For one, they only use their feet to hop up the rocks... so there are lots of "oops" and "ouchs" and "I'm getting the nerve to jump really high." Secondly, it takes some good penguin muscle to waddle 100 yards to its hole in the hill. Way cooler than bugs glowing, tons funnier, and a National Geographic moment for sure.

## Hobbiton and Mordor are Alive and Well in New Zealand

For those of you who are *Lord of the Rings* fans, this place won't disappoint. The whole country seems like it's from a different planet. We would drive for an hour and be in a whole different ecosystem and this happened time and time again. The mountains, the grasslands, the beaches – all look vastly different and just like the movie scenes. I couldn't help but rub my own wedding ring and whisper "My Precious" a few times. Cindy looked weird at me whenever she spotted me doing this... but it's mine... all MINE!

Well, New Zealand is everything they say it is and more. Adventure, nature, craziness, Maori, and Kiwis. I leave you with one thought...

If a Kiwi saw a Kiwi eat a Kiwi, would that be funny or grotesque? Think about that one. Kia Ora!

# Chapter 6: Australia:

## No Worries Mate, If That Doesn't Kill Yah, Something Else Will

Humorous Insights

# In Search of the Great Barrier Reef

You would think that finding the Great Barrier Reef would be an easy task. The reef is hundreds of miles long and right off the coast of Australia. An easy task. Of course, If I am in charge of completing the task, it never ends up being easy. I mean, it's not like you can see the reef from the beach, but you know it is out there... somewhere... I found that it was just getting there that was hard.

Geography lesson: Australia is the fourth largest country in the world. Now I knew Australia was large... I would even say its stinkin' large. Yeah, stinkin'... as in "That's one stinkin' large hump on your back!" or "Stinkin' A... I said you could have a bite, not the whole bloody sandwich!" Australia isn't something you can casually cross. It's a pre-planned journey because it takes hours to get anywhere. And that was my problem, I didn't plan a thing because I didn't realize it was **stinkin'** large. Did I say this already?

Cultural lesson: Australian's call the forest or jungle the "bush." Australians call it the bush because they find it funny when a tourist says, "Bush... that doesn't sound that scary. I'll go for a quick stroll through the 'Bush,'" and the tourist returns without a leg or two.

From Sydney to Cairns, there are at least three types of bush: the thick bush from Sydney to Surfers' Paradise, the subtropical bush from the Gold Coast to Rockhampton, and the grasslands and tropical bush from Mackay to Cairns. We saw them all. How did we do this, you ask?

Rental car, a lot of fuel, and massive patience.

We drove around 2,200 kilometers to see the reef (roughly from Houston, Texas to New York City). Along the way we saw tons of wildlife: kangaroos, echidnas, wombats, and koalas; unfortunately, most of these were roadkill. Yes, koala roadkill. Is that insane or what? Luckily, we did see quite a few live kangaroo in the bush staring at us, making sure we didn't go four-wheeling and make them into floor mats. It was also quite a shocker to see an eight-foot-long snake slither quickly across the road; if I wasn't going a hundred kilometers an hour, I might have not clipped its tail, which didn't slow it down as it avoided the next two cars behind me.

Now, on the map, Mackay (pronounced by Aussies like Mickeye) looks like a perfect place to go scuba diving the reef. Mackay is further up the coast, a bigger city, and on the ocean. So when we pulled up to the tourist office grinning about our much anticipated aquatic adventure and asked where we could get a boat to the Great Barrier Reef, we were expecting all sorts of options. We didn't expect hearing "drive another hour and a half to Airlie Beach!"

What! Didn't the place know we drove for three days through the bush, saw cute fuzzy animals dead on the road, just to get there and now we had to drive more?

Yet serendipity played its part and we found the WhitSunday Islands; a place that Captain Cook sailed through on White Sunday, and thus named the passage for it. The area is pristine, the reef is relatively close and accessible, and best yet... the reef isn't completely destroyed by divers who can barely swim.

Some of you might think, "Why didn't you just go to Cairns, the self-proclaimed capital of diving the Great Barrier Reef?" Well now, that's exactly what we thought too until we researched the distance from Mackay to Cairns and started crying. After 23 hours of driving, we couldn't muster up another nine hours, so we looked for all the anti-Cairns gossip we could rummage up... like, we've heard from tons of people that Cairns is over dived and that the reef has suffered because of it. Tah dah! That's good enough for me... now where do we park?

So... how was the Great Barrier Reef? Let's just put it this way... if you come to Australia and you want to see the Great Barrier Reef, go on a two-to-seven day cruise. I couldn't get enough in the one day I spent there; massive Maori Wrasses, cuddle fish, clown fish, boulder coral, and on and on. Experiences like this just make you want more. It's an unquenchable thirst; just all too enjoyable. Be sure to have that second mortgage ready because you'll need it.

So... it was with a lump in my throat and a tear in my eye that I drove away from this water wonderland. It wasn't until I pulled up to a gas station that I finally could get over my sadness. After filling up the tank with "petrol," I walked to the counter to pay for the fuel. An older gent was behind the register and wore a nametag with "Mick" on it. "G-Day Mate!" was his greeting.

Mick... "G-Day"... that is so funny. Just like in the movie *Crocodile Dundee*. I was in Australia and a guy named Mick said "G-Day."

Now that was priceless.

# Land of the Funny People

I love to laugh. Some people go to movies with me just to hear me laugh at the stupidest movies ever made. Ever seen "Joe Versus The Volcano"? I laughed like a mad man. "Young Frankenstein"? Almost wet my pants. If I die laughing, I will have no complaints.

So, coming to Australia was almost like coming home. Why? 'Cause Aussies have such a great sense of humor. Just to prove it to you, I've assembled a few examples that made me giggle, laugh, or cry from hooting and hollering.

## "Poo-fection Plumbing"

Now this is a guy that loves his crap, literally. He is so comfortable being a plumber that his whole advertising campaign revolves around the word "Poo." Now that is funny; a plumber with poo in his business name. If you don't believe me, look his business up. Whatever the fact, this guy is hilarious... though I have no desire to meet him unless my "loo" is really backed up.

## Road signs that taunt you

This is real. To prove it, I give you pictures. As we drove across Queensland, we found that we were traveling unbelievable distances. All the while, we saw nothing but the "bush" and a lot of road kill. I'm guessing there were a lot of accidents along these highways. I'm also guessing that these accidents come from people falling asleep at the wheel. To counter this, the governing highway boards have put up signs to keep you on your toes. Taunting you and your kids along the way, that's funny.

## Oprah Radio Show

In its last year of production, the Oprah Show decided to go to Australia. Me, I didn't really care until it affected my life. "Oh, are you here with Oprah?" Bloody $#@&! It was not that I didn't like Oprah, she's OK, I just didn't like having every Australian I met asking me if I carried her baggage for a living or was one of the Oprah-Is-My-Life crazies she brought with her. So when I heard a radio program making fun of an Oprah Crazy, I particularly enjoyed it. It was an added bonus that it was hilarious. Well, the crazy lady they made fun of was hysterical to see Oprah in person and the jokes they made about her were hysterical.

Example: "If this lady went crazy for just seeing, not even touching or talking, to Oprah... I mean she went bloody wild... What would this crazy lady do if she saw Jesus or an alien? Probably wet herself and go catatonic!"

That ridiculing was not only funny and on the radio, but it lasted for days.

## Diving

I had always wanted to see the Great Barrier Reef and it was an experience. Loads of fun. What made it funny though was the character I ended up with as a dive partner. Darren was a project manager from Victoria, way down south. When the dive master explained the details of potential shark encounters, Darren decided to supersede the instructions. "No, no, no... If a shark gets close, you stab your partner with a knife and swim away from him as fast as you can." Not funny for me, funny for everyone else. He did try to comfort me after the dive by saying, "You know, if we did see a shark, I wouldn't have had to stick you... the other divers were so stupid, they would have ended up killing themselves... so we would have been fine. No worries Mate!" Classic.

## Lifeguard Outfits

Australian lifeguards wouldn't last a minute in Southern California. Because of their swimming and lifesaving skills? No, they are superb when it comes to those areas. It's their outfits that would get them beat up. Imagine with me now... tight shirts that cut off midriff, tight speedos, yes... speedos, and lastly, and I'm not making this up, beanies. I didn't just exaggerate. I said beanies. They wear beanies. Like the propeller beanies... just without the propellers. Unbelievable. Whoever came up with this idea was a bit plastered at the committee "barbie" (BBQ for us Yanks). "Beanies... yep, I vote they wear beanies. It will distract the drowning bloke long enough to get rescued." And indeed, if I was splashing around, drowning, I would pause upon seeing the speedo–toting-beanie lifeguard and think... "Wow, I am about to die here, but that beanie looks so funny; I can't help laughing." At that point, the lifeguard saves my life. This is the main reason Australian lifeguards are so good at their jobs.

Having spent a good amount of time with Aussies, I think that they are some of the most fun-loving and funny people around. So, next time you find yourselves immersed among Australians... do this social experiment and have a good laugh.

Say, "Aussie Aussie Aussie!" If their response doesn't amuse you, a lifeguard in a speedo and beanie probably won't either.

G'Day, and No Worries!

# That's Not Strange... I'll Show You Strange

One thing you quickly learn living in Australia is that the animals and insects are weirder than anywhere else you have ever been. OK, New Zealand had some weird things going on, but not on the quantity and scale that the Aussies find themselves in.

Normal mammals, what are those? Oh yeah, there are dingoes out there and some dolphins. In general, the whole place is surrounded by marsupials. You know, the mammals that have the underdeveloped fetuses (only an inch or so long) that crawl into the pouches for protection, warmth, and food. What animals, or marsupials, am I talking about? Glad you asked.

Kangaroos, wombats, koalas, wallabies, and wallaroos. These are all marsupials. Crazy, right? What is even stranger is the wombats have upside-down pouches. I guess it comes in handy when they are digging massive holes under houses so the babies don't fall out. These turkeys, I mean wombats, can undermine a house's fountain from the sheer size of the holes they dig. People have survived forest fires by hiding in a wombat's hole, not that it would be my first choice. "Hello Mr. Wombat, I know you can outrun me and tear me to shreds, but I am going to bunker down here while the raging fire passes over head. Why thank you, I will use your fuzzy belly as a pillow... how thoughtful." I then get torn to shreds and thrown into the fire.

Next marsupial, the kangaroo. You ever see kangaroos box? So funny... but so weird. When kangaroos prove their masculinity, they do so by standing tall and swinging left hooks. They could seriously kick someone's butt. That's why most people don't go too close to the male kangaroos. At one of the many zoos we visited, we saw one male roo that kept eyeballing this large Aussie like he wanted a piece of him. It didn't last long, as another male kangaroo came up and they duked it out for a good ten seconds. Bing! Round Over!

Koalas are cute and won't punch you out, but they sleep some eighteen hours a day. Now that is lazy! Shoot, I have worked with directors that did more work than these guys... wait, I take that back... the koalas would win that contest simply on doing nothing since they cause less damage than these leaders. "It was a valiant effort though, good try, massive failure, let's have a celebration."

Koalas kind of stink too. They smell bad for a good reason though, not like teenagers after physical education. Koalas have a scent gland on their chest to mark territory. If they ever woke up, they could defend it. "What, that guy is in my tree... can't he smell that tree is mine? Bloody bloke is going to get a fist full... yawn... but maybe later... zzzzz."

What's also weird? Platypuses. They can't get any stranger. Lays eggs, looks like a science project gone wrong with the duck bill, fish feet, and beaver body. Only Looney Tunes could think of sticking those parts together, which reminds me, didn't Daffy Duck end up as a platypus in one of the shows? Most thought platypuses were extinct because they are so hard to see in the wild. I think this is a lie, and it is just that no one wanted to be remotely close to them. With wombats and kangaroos beating everyone up, one can't take a chance even with the ones that look harmless.

Now, has anyone ever seen a cassowary? I know it is not a marsupial or a mammal, but it wins the weirdo contest in Australia. Ostriches look cute next to these. Of course Australia has their own version of ostriches called emus, which are from the ugly cousin side of the bird family; you know, the one no one likes to be reminded about. "Shh, shut it Junior, we're in pleasant company who don't need to know about Cousin Albert's six toes and three ears." Sorry, back to the cassowaries. These birds have the head of a dinosaur and the body of a bird. Now the head... how to say this gently... is wacko! Some type of hard-ridged fin on top of a blue, red, and orange neck. These things stare at you close up... like, an "I want to butt head you for looking at me like that" stare. Cassowaries have to be the punk rock species of the animal kingdom. Always mad for no reason, trying to pick a fight with you 'cause you're a nerd, calling you names... augh... sorry, high school relapse. I don't appreciate all the cassowaries ganging up and poking fun of me. Rude animals.

I wouldn't do the insect kingdom justice if I didn't mention that Australian insects are all big here. After thousands of years roaming this huge continent, they grew to small-animal size. This phenomenon was proven to us one morning when we found Elizabeth hiding under her sheets in the front room where the hide-a-bed lay. When we questioned her why she had all the blankets on top of her, she simply poked an arm out and pointed to the ceiling. Above the blinds lay a huntsman spider, basically a tarantula with long legs. As a grown male, I almost squealed. That's when everyone deserted me in other rooms while I tamed the mighty beast. I almost wet myself... luckily, I had a shotgun and lots of knives. Humans 1, Insects 0. Next time, however, we run for it.

Now we can't forget that Australia has ten of the most venomous snakes in the world. Luckily, only a couple people get killed every year from snake bites. The anti-venom is good stuff. The people that croak from bites usually are running from bush fires, step on the snakes tail, get bit, fall into a wombat hole... and we all know what happens then... yep, gets the sheez beaten out of them by kangaroos. And no one wants to be seen in public after you get thumped by a kangaroo... that's just embarrassing.

# Chapter 7:  Singapore and Malaysia:

# Buddha, Buddha, Buddha, Bless my Fooda, Fooda, Fooda

Humorous Insights

# Singapore - The City of the Future

Engineers are a strange bunch. I feel confident that I can even call the vast majority bizarre. It is my professional liberty to call engineers names because I am one. And nothing gets an engineer more excited than a good calculator... I mean, cool gadgets and gizmos, impressive buildings, mass transportation's schedule that operates to the second, and of course, escalators.

Okay, there might be a few engineers out there that don't get excited about these things, though I question if they truly are engineers and not just science majors with engineering titles. Don't get mad you science majors out there, we engineers need you for testing purposes. So please stand very still, this shouldn't hurt for long.

Singapore is an engineer's dream. Not only is the name easy to remember (sing-a-pore) but the place is both a city and a country. How many places can you say that about? Love the simplicity. "What country you going to?" "Singapore." "Really, what city in Singapore?" "Singapore." The circular humor is amazing.

Singapore is a fast moving, constantly adjusting, metropolitan monster. Fifty years ago, there wasn't a building more than 10 stories tall. Now the place is loaded with skyscrapers, manufacturing, and banks - okay, banks don't get me excited – grumble...grumble...bank...grumble. It's not just that Singapore has tall buildings, it's how they built them and why they built them that impresses me.

It starts with Yin and ends with Yang... or does it go it starts with Feng and ends with Shui? Either way, as I told my youngest daughter after dinner, "No, you can't keep the chopsticks, you'll get more tomorrow... Yep, tomorrow... How do I know? 'Cause there's chopsticks out the Yin Yang here!" Now I thought that was pretty funny... chopsticks out the Yin Yang. Whole bunch of Asians... chopsticks... ok, give me some leeway here, I'm an engineer.

Well, to a Singaporean, you can't just make a tall building. You have to make it super tall (that's hard but doable), satisfy Chinese superstition and luck (wait, that's a bit much), make it in harmony with Nature with Feng Shui (Crap! Now you're pushing it), and then make it architecturally amazing to the eye and imagination (I quit! I only make ugly skyscrapers that look like building blocks. Find the dude that made the Sydney Opera House if you want creative). Give it ten escalators, too.

Yet, you find these skyscrapers everywhere - not the building block ones (although you do find a few of those (the engineer won that discussion, hehe)) - but you find the skyscrapers that have grass growing on the walls, trees on the roof, and bushes mathematically arranged in a logarithmic pattern. A taxi driver told me Singapore is called the "Garden City." He was definitely right. And I almost forgot, escalators that lead to more escalators.

Another thing that amazes me about Singapore is the shopping malls. How can you have one gigantic mall right next to another gigantic mall... that happens to be right next to another gigantic mall? Shopping is a pastime here - and that isn't an exaggeration, it is over the top. Take "Iluma." It's a mall close to where we were staying. This mall specializes in Japanese, Chinese, and Korean imports (isn't everything from Japan, China, and Korea anyway?). The construction is abstract, the exterior glows with lights that make patterns, and there are trees on the third and fifth floors. Did I mention it has escalators?

Now you might think I'm crazy for admitting this, but the National Singapore Library, which is 15 stories above ground (3 or 4 below), is a skyscraper and it has 15 stories of escalators. Yep, 15 stories of these mechanical, moving steps. I had to go up every one of them just because, like I said, there were 15 stories of escalators! It only took about 20 minutes or so to go to the top with minor, "holy smoke" moments that we paused for. How can you have a "holy smoke" moment in a library, you say? Well, around the 10th floor - a good 15 minutes of riding the escalator - we noticed books behind glass. We had to find out why. Well, the books are really old. How old? Try about 1000 years old! A few of them were made in the Ming Dynasty. Yeah, that even sounds old. Enough of the gawking, kids, we have to get back to the escalators.

It really is baffling what this small country has done. Singapore has a vision of being the city of the future. They have a great start to it, and if they keep making more of what they're making, it'll be really fun to come back. And no, it won't be just for the escalator rides either.

Okay, maybe only partially for the escalators... blame it on the bizarre engineer in me.

Let's ride.

# Malaysia - Indiana Jones' Winter Home

Coming from Singapore, Malaysia seems a few years behind the times, but oddly enough, just as advanced. How can I say that? It could be my Jedi knight capabilities, or my Ninja intuition, possibly my master intellect, or just my God given talent of vision.

What?! What did you just say? You're saying I have talent? Why, thank you. I'll take any compliment given, even if it is only about my eye sight.

Malaysia could be described as being in a race with itself. The country wants to be a manufacturing giant (which it really is already), an advanced engineering location (working on it), and a "Who's who of modern Asia" (I'd give it a thumbs up). However, what makes Malaysia so interesting is not their race to become a technology hub, it is Malaysia's ability to make the common man (or woman) into Indiana Jones. Yep... I felt more like a whipping, gun-slinging archeologist than an astronaut or brainiac.

Of course, any good "Indie" wannabe needs loads of practice with the following Malaysian staples. So, get your passport, your hat, and your whopping sense of adventure and get going on your persona.

<u>Taxi Drivers</u> - Any good action movie has great car chases. Malaysia has cities chuck-full of race and stunt car drivers. They are called taxi drivers. These road ragers have no fear; they seem to laugh at the old game of "playing chicken," you know, see who flinches first. The center line? For people not courageous enough to drive perfectly centered on the dashed line. Need a quick getaway? Wave a taxi down on any street, they're everywhere. Just make sure their meters work or you'll be needing a quick getaway from your quick getaway.

<u>Weird Food Stands</u> - If you can't eat spicy food... well, you're not trying hard enough. If you get indigestion, you've just started. If

you almost soil your pants, you're just beginning to be adventurous. Indiana doesn't eat potatoes on the road, he eats... shoot, whatever looks the weirdest. In Malaysia, you will have plenty of opportunity to test out your taste buds, sample exotic flare, and challenge your very soul as you pray at the foot of your porcelain throne. Yep, pointing at something on the street can grow some serious hair on your chest... and some serious fire and smoke out your...

<u>Shops With Weapons</u> - You can find anything in Malaysia. Need a movie that's in the theaters? DVD stores everywhere. Need a Gucci purse or a Prada bag? Only 30 ringgits. And yes, of course it's the genuine article. Need one big honking sword? Right next to the watch stand. Guns, whips, grenades, you can find those in Colombia. As for swords though, or the Malaysian Kris... no problem. What size do you need? Toothpick sized, dagger, sword, club, we have it all. Of course, now that I think of it... Indiana Jones always shot the guy with the honking big sword with his pistol. Rats, oh well... How's your aim?

<u>Monkeys</u> – Go to the Batu Caves outside of Kuala Lumpur and they will steal your keys from your back pocket. Be careful though as the monkeys don't practice the best hygiene. Watch monkeys long enough and you see that they pick any bodily orifice and eat anything even slightly edible. Indiana loves monkeys and you will too. Just don't bend over with your back turned... 'cause they will pick your....

<u>Snakes</u> - Can't go to Malaysia if you can't tolerate a few snakes. Don't worry though. They are usually in cages. You are an Indiana Jones wannabe though so snakes should be second nature. You should walk right up to that cage, take a good look inside, and scream like a little girl because you're scared to death of snakes. So why the heck are you so close to that stupid thing anyway?

Everything else an Indiana wannabe needs is here too. Chinese sidekick - though I'm sure labor laws will force you to hire someone at least 16 years old. Rickshaw - comes with bicycles now, but its close enough for our purposes. Getting beat up - can't comment on that one, but I'm sure you can think of your own training... just don't overdo it since they have the death penalty still.

Well, you have all the tools now to be a whipping, gun-toting, adventure prone, jungle master. While in Malaysia, you can hone your talents and skills while running around both the city and the forest jungles.

Last words of advice though. First, make sure you get your keys back from the monkey; second, make sure your sidekick doesn't kick your side; and lastly, make sure your taxi driver doesn't scare the bowels outta you while driving. You already have a sensitive stomach from lunch. And whatever that was, it was mega spicy.

# Malaysia - Grow Hair on Your Chest, Just Like Mom Said

Do you remember your Mom telling you, "Eat your broccoli, it will grow hair on your chest?" Or, "Liver is good for you, it will grow hair on your chest?" Does anyone eat liver anymore? Anyway, where am I going here? Oh, right... It seems that every time there is something to eat that may be an unpleasant experience, mothers try to convince their young males that by simply eating this object, follicles of hair will spontaneously erupt slap dab on their chest. Why? Who knows. Do I care? Absolutely.

Of the many genetic dominating characteristics present in my family, chest hair is something we don't brag about. In fact, it has become something of an embarrassment. Ask my brother, who has so few chest hairs he was able to pluck them. Yes, pluck them! It must have taken around 15 seconds to pull all six of them.

Malaysia is known for its variety of food. Chinese, Indian, Malay, Filipino, Thai, Japanese, and of course, American (in the form of Pizza Hut, McDonalds, KFC, and Burger King).

Malaysia is also known because of the variety of eating locations: full blown restaurants, mid-sized dining areas, and yard-sale plastic picnic tables by the side of the road. The food is usually cheap (good start), usually hot (now we're talking), and contains items that I knew would generate a heap of hair on my chest (we have a winner).

So, the experiment was executed over the course of three weeks. The things I do for science.

My first medical dose came at a food stand in the Central Market in Kuala Lumpur. The stand was cute, well organized, clean, and looked "official." What does official mean? It was a chain store, stand, booth... whatever. Though it only had one employee, the operation moved smoothly and we all got our food quickly. The food was simple and tasty. All in all, a fun meal. Until around 3 AM, that's when the bathroom calls began. Walls were thin that night... way too thin. We have to laugh now, but we sure weren't laughing as we lined up to use the facilities.

The second dose came eating at a skewer stand in Chinatown. These stands have everything on skewers, you pick what you want to eat, and they either grill it for you or you dunk it in the boiling water tub that centers your table. Here is the dilemma. I stared at dozens of selections of "food" and couldn't identify one thing. Imagine this selection of food on skewer sticks. "What's this?" "Chicken." "What's this?" "Fish." "What's this?" "Pork." Problem. I pointed to the same stick three times. What to do? Pick one of everything and pretend to know what you're doing. This event ended much better than dose number one and the food was fantastic.

Visiting the Batu Caves introduced the third hair producing dose... Indian food. As I looked at the menu, I quickly realized that I was in the hands of people that I not only don't know, but if I somehow ticked them off, I quite possibly would end up eating something... well, "unnatural." The menu luckily had pictures that assisted as we negotiated our order, strategically using phrases like "No Spicy" and "This Have Meat?" and my personal favorite "You eat first, I eat second." As I looked at our daughters' faces, I knew that this was a moment of truth... "Is Dad going to poison us with green stuff that should be yellow and red stuff that should be brown?"

The fourth dose came in Penang. Georgetown, the main city on the island of Penang, is famous for its hawker stands. What is a hawker stand? A hawker stand is usually a wok, a fire, and one insanely fast, cooking Malaysian. The stands can come in a few sizes, such as small, really small, and so small that the fire is catching your clothes on fire. To get your food, you simply walk up to a stand, point at the concoction they're making, grunt the number of orders you want (I prefer the "Aung - Aung" counting style as opposed to the "Duh - Duh" one used throughout the nomad sections of Duh U No Aung Nada). The cook will put the fire out on their sleeve, gesture you to a table, and whip up whatever they think you just ordered. What arrives is a mystery, a culinary treat, and usually – and may I add, surprisingly – tasty. Just because it might have tasted good did not stop me from praying to the rather large Buddha statue on the wall. "Please Mr. Buddha, save me from what this lady just made me. I know it is chicken, or pork, or that dog that's been missing the last couple of days... just make sure it doesn't come back up - or out - too quickly. Thanks."

What I failed to explain in detail was that even though I suggested only four doses, the dose range was well over 40 in number. Each day represented another opportunity to test the taste buds, challenge the bowels, and increase my faith in a superior being. Food in Malaysia definitely was a mental, physical, and spiritual experience.

Of course, you're wondering... "If this is all about chest hair, how much hair do you now have on your chest?"

Well, that's just a little personal, wouldn't you say? However, I will give you a clue... Malaysia is home to the "Man of the Jungle," which translates into Malay as the word "Orangutan."

# Chapter 8: Thailand:

# You Like Little Spicy, Spicy, or Thai Spicy?

Humorous Insights

# Disneyland for Grown-Ups

Sucker!

Yep, that's what you'd call me. A sucker through and through. And why would you call me names? Because I can't get enough of Disneyland. I love the rides, the characters, the food, the smell and yes, I love the "magic" of the whole place. Going to this park reminds me of my younger years – happy times when my brothers and sister weren't trying to kill me. You might make fun of me, call me names and laugh at my Mickey Mouse hat. I really don't care. The insults won't work.

"What? You're done? Great! Come on kids, load up, Mom is finally done making fun of Dad."

Waiting in lines, people acting crazy, getting gypped on souvenirs, entertainment around every corner. Sounds like Disneyland, you say? Yes, but what I'm talking about now is Thailand.

It's amazing, just when you thought you had seen it all, a new country pulls out their Ace card and slams it down in front of you. By now I should be used to it. I just can't believe anyone or any country can get any more entertaining than the last place. And how Thailand reminds me of my favorite theme park is really easy to figure out. But I'll help you out, put the pieces together, part the clouds of smog and soot that cover Bangkok... Cough... Cough... Choke!

Did you know that Thailand is a kingdom? Crazy, huh? Like a Magic Kingdom? No, that's crazy talk. But it is a kingdom! They have a king, a queen, and like 500 sons, grandsons, great-grandsons that are in line for the throne. If you don't know the name of the king, that's no problem. I still don't know it. However, if I saw him on the street buying a bowl of Tom Yam or Massaman soup, I would definitely recognize him. The Thai king's portrait is on coins, bills, and about a billion 50 foot tall signs around the country.

Someone not recognizing the king of Thailand, while they are in Thailand, is like someone going to a Disney park and saying "What's with the gigantic mouse?" You'll get beat up in Disney by Pluto and dragged to death behind a gang of Tuk Tuks in Bangkok.

Speaking of Tuk Tuks, they are the new rollercoasters in Bangkok. They're not necessarily new, and they don't run on tracks, but the acrobatic show they put you through is just as fun as any coaster ride you have ever been on. My girls laughed harder and longer on our 15 minute Tuk Tuk ride than they ever did on the Dumbo ride. For me, it's much more thrilling. I mean, danger is assumed on Space Mountain or Thunder Mountain, but I know deep down nothing is going to happen. Engineers and lawyers get my point. On a Tuk Tuk ride, you have no idea if you will survive the next turn, let alone the entire ride. And if by chance you do live through the entire journey, you've laughed, cried, shouted, screamed, and wet yourself (lucky for you 7-11 stores in Thailand carry disposable underwear next to the candy section). "Yes, a Twix bar, a spicy pork with sticky rice sandwich, and a pack of undies."

There's a strange breed of folk that roam around Thailand just like in amusement parks. Ever notice? Wandering the streets. Dressed all weird. Asking stupid questions in strange languages. Looking lost and confused. They can be swindled into almost anything. Like paying 200 Baht for a Thailand stamped pencil holder. I'm talking about crazy people. Everywhere. And they're called tourists. Amazing specimens – should be charged to get into places. Like to see a 5.5 ton solid gold Buddha in a sitting position. Wait a sec, I got charged to see a solid gold Buddha. Do I ask stupid questions, dress funny? Moving right along...

Impossible I say... Impossible! It simply can't be done. No human being can walk down Thai streets and not be entertained. No matter your profession, your hobbies, your likes or dislikes, Thai people are entertaining to watch when they work, play, sit around, ride the bus, whatever they do.

They take professions to the max too. I witnessed with my own two eyes (20-10 vision, mind you) a shop that sells bolts. *Only bolts!* Long ones, small ones, thick ones – a whole shop for bolts. And by the look of things, the shop has been open for years.

Not amazed, how about balancing your whole family of five on a scooter motorcycle and still have the groceries in tow? How about a father with his four daughters crammed on his scooter and the daughters all grinning ear to ear because of the slurpees they each had in hand? How about an 80-year-old lady hauling two baskets of fruits and veggies between a long pole that she was supporting on her shoulders? You just don't see this stuff! Though I do want to try out the five-person scooter stunt – that sounds like the making of a good story or an expensive medical bill.

If you want food, Thailand is the right place for you. This is no simple amusement park catering service. You can walk 50 feet, eat something from a hawker stand, walk another 50 feet, eat something else from a different hawker stand. You can do this for miles. This may be a long shot, but I'm willing to bet (and I'm no betting man) my favorite pair of shoes (the Australian flip-flops - not my 3 year old Nikes) that you could eat non-stop from one side of Thailand to the other side and not go more than a half-mile without finding a place to eat.

Thai people are professionals too. Crack of dawn type people. Serious about ingredients, spices, textures, cleanliness... er, maybe cleanliness... the verdict is still out on if that stomach bout of pure nastiness was from the Pad Thai at the hawker stand, the plate that was washed in the bucket by the hawker stand, or the 7-11 tuna rice ball that I choked down. Needless to say, Thais know what they are doing and they do it with precision. True professionals.

Thailand has to be souvenir-land. Second to no one, not even the Magic Kingdom. Funny thing is, you can buy just as many Mickey Mouse or Donald Duck t-shirts in Bangkok as you could in California. Though they do look a little off. Maybe the bad silk screening. Maybe it's because they spelled Mickey Mouse as "Mikey Moose." My point is that you can buy Thai souvenirs in every form possible. You think you're spending a fortune on stuff too, 2,000 Baht here, 550 Baht there. It's very nerve racking until you remember that 1,000 Baht is roughly 33 US dollars. "Cindy, go crazy! ...well, have fun, I mean... you know, with a little fun and a lot of restraint... can I have that 4,000 Baht back?"

And of course, you can't have a good park without pirates... and Thailand has their fair share of pirates. Not talking about the "Argghh!" pirates, I'm talking about the "Only 300 Baht to hotel... give you discount." Then you find out the taxi ride should have cost only 70 Baht. "PIRATES!!!" These masters of the con come in all sorts of shapes and sizes. "Buy birds... set free... bring good luck!" Such a novel thing to do. Then you see the sign down the path that suggests I just aided a group that specializes in animal terrorism. "PIRATES... ARGH!" The old lady swash-buckled me! Buy two of this ice cream, three of that type... "How much? 175 Baht? OK." Walk down the street... "Wait a second... that only should have cost 155 Baht! Arggh, that lily-livered scallywag hornswoggled me! Dirty PIRATES!"

As you can see, adventure awaits the eager folk that are ready to journey to Thailand's shores. There is something for every kid at heart. You will be neither disappointed nor down-hearted. It just can't happen.

Thailand is a place of magic, a destination for food lovers, a refuge from modern, structured society, an escape to beaches of blue waters and tropical fish, and the best, darn amusement park a grown-up can visit in today's world...

...and that is coming from one of the world's biggest kids-at-heart too. "Argh! Now step aside matey... I'm the captain of this here's Tuk Tuk... and I'm th' one that'll be setting it a sailing. HAHAHA"

I'm a sucker for stuff like this.

# Help... I'm Being Held Captive By My Taxi Driver

We've had our share of being on the wrong end of the stick when it comes to taxi drivers. Usually we get to our destination, pay the driver, and never see him again. Then, there are the taxi drivers that you will never forget. Mainly because they trick you into a money scheme or something similar and you spend all your energy trying to get out of it and it becomes a memory you never forget even though you really want to - specifically because you feel like a dope for falling for the whole thing.

The following is an actual, accurate, and somewhat detailed description of such an event that I personally experienced - and barely survived - and it all started with a taxi driver.

(zoom into the past... swish, swish, lightning, lightning... you know, for added effect)

Chiang Mai, Thailand. Religious, commercial, calm Chiang Mai. Wats are everywhere in Chiang Mai. You could step from one Wat roof to the next Wat roof... and barely touch a Tuk Tuk. We were visiting one of the most spectacular Thai Buddhist temples, or Wats, around. As we finished enjoying the large Naga dragons and massive golden Buddha, a taxi driver was waiting outside and offered to take us wherever we wanted. He looked like he was 10, though it's hard to say because 80-year-old Thais look like they're 20 (must be the water... which I refuse to drink. Not worth the risk of a digestive disaster). He started with a simple truth, "Where you going handsome, tall man?"

Well, I am really tall, but I wasn't fazed at all. I ignored the kindergarten-sized driver and debated with my wife on what to do since the Saturday night market didn't start till it was dark.

"Go see another Wat, I guess." I was out of ideas.

Amber started choking herself, Sophia poked herself in the eyes, Elizabeth just started crying.

"Ok, OK! We won't go see another Wat... we'll go to McDonalds and get ice cream cones."

"Yeah", the three cried out.

"I'm joking... we're going to another Wat! And this time, no asking questions about Monk hygiene... it's embarrassing."

Cindy saved the kids by suggesting an alternative, "Let's just go to that silverware factory in Long Dong"... or Hang Dong... Kong Dong... Dong something or other. Anyway, it was a great way to stop the kids from jumping in front of a motorcycle.

So, we're back at the Thai taxi driver that uses blocks to touch the gas pedal.

"How much to see silverware factory?"

"Ga ga goo goo... 100 Baht." His English wasn't great but I understood 100 Baht. I seem to have understood also "give you good deal since you so strong." True, true, it was a good deal.

"Ok... let's ride."

Now, Chiang Mai is famous for the artisan crafts - everything is made here. From silverware, to umbrellas, to jade elephant pendants that you pay way too much for and you feel stupid for buying them because the half-blind lady has them at her night market stand for a third the price... so stupid... I should have known it... but they had A/C... I was weak... and they are cute elephants.

The place to find stuff in Chiang Mai is in a suburb called Bo Sang. Not to be confused with the other suburb, factory selling town of Yu Suk Big Time - that's for sure a tourist trap, I mean, who is that stupid to go to Yu Suk Big Time and buy something? I mean you really have to be a complete loser to fall for that trap.

Getting out of the sun, the heat, the humidity, even getting away from those pests that suck your blood out of you, commonly called mosquitoes (I prefer the more formal name - attorney bugs), was worth the ride. It was so pleasant to be seated in A/C that when we arrived at the stop, I didn't even notice it was a jewelry store.

"You sure this is the silverware factory?"

"I poo poo diaper... you visit store."

Yikes... ok, let's visit the large, glassed, jewelry store.

Jewelry is a very well-known scam in Thailand. Every Tuk Tuk driver in Bangkok has a friend "Bruce Lee" that will give you a great "kick in the face" deal on necklaces. The problem is you have no idea how much a ruby necklace costs. I mean, when was the last time you bought your wife a diamond necklace or a precious stone ring - something really nice - something she will love you forever for, something... err... man... it's been a long time (awkward moment pause)... That's why you end up doing something irrational like, "if it costs 15,000 Baht... divide by 30, that makes it 5, carry the zeros... like 500 US bucks, what a bargain. It was 15,000 seconds ago and now it's only 500. I'll take 3." Then they cry that you could get the same thing on Ebay for $80 and they'll throw a couple jade elephant pendants on top of the deal just to be nice. You can try to complain to the police - and they may help you if they can stop laughing at you long enough to write the report.

We made it out alive and only had three of those overpriced, miniature, probably fake jade, probably get lost or stolen, elephant pendants.

The taxi driver, new diaper and all, was drinking a cold one, relaxing in the car.

"Not this silverware store, the other silverware store. You know, the one with silver in it? Shiny, shiny, silver, you know? Siiiiillllll-vvveeerrrr?"

"Oh oh... Siver-waw... auh auh... goo goo." He gives me the thumbs up... probably some vulgarity in Thai that warrants me poo pooing in my own diaper.

The next place had silver... but no silverware. Lots and lots of silver bowls, silver Buddhas, silver candle stick holders (does anyone really need solid silver candle stick holders these days?) "Igor... get me the candle sticks, we must go to the tower during this lightning storm." Come on, let's get with the times... now the silver nun-chucks, those are a must have.

We find our taxi driver with another cold one, feet (size 1 booties) kicked up on the table - shoot, this guy gets a drink everywhere we end up. So strange. We ended this factory quicker than he planned because he tried to reroute us back inside.

"You not see this side."

"That's because we want to see a silverware factory... not a kashmir rug outlet. Silverware... fork, knife, spoon... eating stuff." It's hard to explain some things in pantomime. Sticking three fingers into the air, trying to resemble a fork, got him to flip me off... pretending to eat got the other taxi drivers gut barrel laughing... "No... not elephant... no, not monkey... silverware."

120

"This silverware store." He obviously hasn't seen the one we saw just two days ago.

We climbed into the taxi, he drove across the road, and we ended up at what looked like a Communist party rally building that happened to survive multiple bombing raids by the Tuk Tuk association for jewelry store owners. But it was something new.

"Cindy, I found the silverware!" There was one set of dull looking forks and spoons, 4 pieces in all. The rest of the shop had Buddhas, pots, necklaces, and yes, candle stick holders. We were so tired; we ended up walking opposite of the hundred Chinese tourists moving through the store.

"Wrong way... store this way," a store worker exclaimed as I walked to the back of the store.

"We look at factory, no look at store, we want silverware..." and we walked out the back door.

Our taxi driver barely had time to crack open the cold beverage he just was given, "Another drink... what the heck is going on?"

"OOO... gaaa... Auh." He obviously wanted to know why we left so quickly.

"We want to go back to Saturday Night Market. No more silverware. We buy in China."

His face went blank and you could tell he was about to ask us something he was uncomfortable asking.

"Please... one more store... 5 minutes... no buy anything... need one more store for gas coupon."

"AAAH HAAA! I knew it was a scam. Just like Cancun and that free breakfast, and Vegas and that free hotel stay, and Miami and that free cruise, and... wow, this isn't sounding good. Have I been cheated by everyone?"

Amber nods, Sophia agrees, Elizabeth even whispers "Yip." I look at Cindy.

"It's alright, dear... it's quite endearing."

Endearing doesn't get me those two and a half hours of my life back, or the other 30 minutes I spent making the Kashmir rug guy believe I was going to buy something huge and at the last second pretending I had one already and didn't need one anymore. Poor guy fell on his carpet and cried, cried hard, cried like a 10-year-old taxi driver not getting his free drink from the factory store because we came out too fast.

But that's life in Bo Sang.

And I'm happy to say that we negotiated our kidnapping taxi ride to conclusion. And cost us only 100 Baht. But we were alive, A/C cooled, and ready for the Saturday Night Market.

Unfortunately, we found no silverware, bought no forks, no spoons, and no knives...

But those candle sticks holders will go great with the solid silver Buddha... sounds like time for a cold one.

# Tigers and Elephants

It's fun watching the kids get excited about seeing animals in the wild. We saw quite a bit along the way. In South America, we saw animals really close in a zoo. In Costa Rica, we got close to animals since they were swinging in the trees. In Australia, we fed them in animal refuges. However, in Thailand, we not only fed them, we sat by them, touched them, and played with them - it's a whole new level. It's on a level that not only the kids loved, but the adults too.

We started with tigers. Shoot, why not, right? The tiger handlers guided us into a cage and quickly locked it behind us. The trainer smiled at us through his half mouth of teeth, we made a double take at him and openly wondered, "Wait a sec... did he only have one arm?" I didn't know if they lock us up to protect us or the tigers. Whichever way, it was a bit unnerving.

The girls went with the two-month-old tigers. Sissy stuff if you ask me. Seriously, if these tigers went nuts on us, they could have only bitten a few fingers off. If I was going to get mauled, I wanted it to be by something large enough it would have been impressive. Make me a man, not a pansy.

You disagree?

Imagine with me here. You go somewhere, anywhere. Someone sees the large scar on your arm. "What the crap happened to you?" "Oh, this?" you respond back. "I got it in Thailand playing with tigers." Your new admirer looks it over and asks, "Must have hurt. How big was the tiger?" Your nose twists, you begin to blush, "About the size of a medium dog." No longer an admirer, the passerby continues, "A medium dog? How old?" Gulp... "Er... three months." This all concludes with pulling your two-inch ego off the ground as your nemesis laughs and walks away.

Sissy stuff.

That was why I chose the biggest tiger with which they allowed humans to interact. If they had a tiger that was known to chew bodybuilders into two pieces, that would be the one I would have picked... for... for pictures. My tigers, yes two, were like 500 pounds each, claws larger than my face, teeth bigger than most dinner knives. *Manly tigers.*

Sitting by a tiger is amazing. If you get a trainer that thinks he's Thailand's newest prodigy in photography, the experience becomes mind bending. I'm telling you, I was the prop in a tiger photo shoot. "Sit here, lay here, grab his tail, he likes that." On the whole, it was really funny... until the trainer brought out the chicken pieces and toy bell. The bell got the tiger excited and the chicken got it hungry. It's only a shame the piece of flung chicken missed me - I was looking forward to a set of parallel scars on my chest. That would not only be a good story to top my firemen brothers' burning buildings stuff, but something manly I could show off at parties. "You call that a scar? Look at this!" [Rip open my shirt like superman] It would have been awesome.

So to top this experience, I needed to find an animal that would be just as impressive as a tiger encounter in Thailand... and that would be an elephant.

Elephants have been a symbol of Thailand for as long as "Siam" has been in existence. It's not that surprising since elephants are quite formidable: Long tusks, large bodies, and trunks. Anyone would be awestruck looking at one eye-to-eye, face-to-trunk. This was perfect.

Besides an elephant, what other animal has a trunk? An anteater - doesn't really look like a trunk, more of a big snout. I can't think of one, and the trunk of the elephant is everything. You take away the trunk of an elephant and all you have left is a tall, weird hippo. The elephant trunk is also what an elephant utilizes for everything.

For example, an elephant uses his trunk to paint, grab stuff, smell, shoot water at you, spit (or was that snot? It was gross, whatever it was), play a harmonica, place hats on peoples' heads, and about anything else you can imagine. The trunk is like a multi-purpose veggiematic. "It slices, it dices, it makes julienne fries... it can even blow coconuts like cannonballs." Ok, I saw that last bit from a Saturday morning cartoon, but everything else I've seen with my own eyes. 20/10 vision, remember?

As a family, we saw all of this in Chiang Mai and Ayutthaya, Thailand. Elephants have lost almost their entire natural habitat so there are farms now, or elephant refuges, that take care of these massive animals. They teach them tricks in order to earn money to feed them. And feeding them is an effort all in itself.

We bought a few bundles of sugarcane. One elephant ate the whole bundle in one crunch, stock and all. If I'm right, it was "grab, crunch, swallow." Super-fast and three dollars down the toilet. So, I had to be smarter than the elephant. I bought a bundle of bananas (I know, elephants eat bananas too - wonder what the monkeys think about that food invasion). I then proceeded to individually separate the bananas and the kids gave the bananas one by one to them.

You could tell in their beady eyes that they weren't impressed by my new plan. One by one, the bananas were thrown into their mouths. Not even a crunch with these, just pure swallowing. At the end of this food-harassment-game, I was convinced that this elephant was plotting my demise. How do I know this? He pointed his trunk at me, passed it then under his throat, and made a "Skeeechhh" noise. Like a pirate!

Now this was my kind of animal... no messing around at mealtime, had a talent with paints, had a massive form with killer tusks... and the idea hit me like a ton of elephant dung.

I've decided to adopt an elephant and become a superhero. It's unbelievable that no one has thought of this before. You can't get any cooler than a superhero. And girls love elephants. It's a perfect combo. Cindy would love it...

Amazing stories to tell, a clever animal to tease your Yorkie with, the neighbors would never think of messing with you (too scared that you'd knock their house over), invitations to kids birthday parties... and don't forget about all the superhero stuff: action figures, comic books, TV shows.

"SuperPhant and the Amazing Ricardo!"

OK... the name needs work, but you can't deny, it's all really manly!

# Chapter 9: China:

# These Guys Have Been Around For How Long?

# Hong Kong - Fake Watches and Tailored Suits

You'd think that being a professional in business for so many years, that I would love having a nice, tailored suit and a spiffy-looking watch. That way I can walk around and feel good about my appearance and myself. However, if you think anything like me, you understand that people get buried in their nice, tailored suits and expensive watches. So I would rather have a t-shirt, shorts, and sneakers and pretend that I'm not getting old. Sport the clothing of youth and warm weather.

Now enter Hong Kong...

It doesn't get more metropolitan than Hong Kong. Fantastic skyscrapers, unbelievably efficient metro, double-decker street rail and buses, restaurants on every corner... oops, that's 7-11. The city is so easy to get around that it would take a special person to get lost... and to answer your question, I only got lost once... and it was in a very poorly designed metro station. Completely not my fault.

So when we arrive at any new place, I prefer to spend the first day walking around. See the lay of the land. Get my bearings. Sense how things run and where places are. This roaming approach has worked wonders wherever we have gone. Not only does it allow me to see where general things are (grocery stores, post office, restaurants), but walking around for hours helps me get the kids excited about whatever my pea-brain has concocted for the family to do. If I get complaints from the troops about the agenda, I simply remind them that we can easily go back to walking around for eight hours like "yesterday" and they immediately are perfectly willing to see how petroleum is converted into seven different organic compounds.

There are some downfalls to walking around a lot... as I found out in Hong Kong.

Here's the scenario: The streets are crowded. Not just crowded but swamped. People walking, people standing around, people talking, and then there are those who are just waiting to sell some unsuspecting person whatever they can... and it is usually a "copy watch" or a "tailored suit."

At first I kindly said, "No thanks." Then, after a hundred or so watch and suit salesmen had accosted me, I began pretending they weren't there. You know, thinking the whole time, "walk past... no eye contact, no eye contact... hurry now he's getting close, look the other way... made it alive. Big smile, big breath of air, oh no... Here comes another one."

Of course, ignoring these salesmen didn't work for that long.

On day two, I resorted to full-blown Kung Fu. The whole scene was just like a Hong Kong movie, one lone fighter against hundreds of mean-looking guys that have nothing better to do than beat up a Kung Fu master. The aftermath was a mess. Business cards here and there... teeth littering the concrete... grown men crying... and a few fake Rolex watches and a couple tailored suits worse for wear.

Well, it's not good to go all "Kick To Duh Face" on people, so I developed the "Anti-Fake Watch and Tailored Suit Kick In Duh Face" defense program (also named AFWATSUKIDUFA... for short, you know, so that you can easily remember it... it's a great marketing scheme and looks great in Chinese characters). The best part is I'm giving this great program away free; simply to rid the streets of Hong Kong of these faceless combatants. No child in Hong Kong, or Kowloon for that matter, should be mentally bruised as they watch their fathers Kung Fu in the streets over "fitted or pleated" pants.

The first part of AFWATSUKIDUFA is called "Be Nice Back." These guys are treated quite poorly, so you need to surprise them by being just as nice back to them as they are to you. Not only will this freak them out, it puts you in control of the psychological warfare.

Part two of AFSUDU (just decided to shorten it... hard to type and all) is referred to as "No, You Listen." The fake watch dudes have a pitch they say countless times a day. You have them stumbling by being nice, now you start talking to maintain conversation control. You accomplish this by talking loudly and staring at them eye-to-eye.

The third stage of AS-UD-FA (didn't like AFSUDU... trying another spin at the name) is to close the deal by using my favorite technique "Buy My Old Watch." Critical to the close out of this phase is to reverse roles and try and sell your old watch to the "new fake" watch guy. You have to believe that you will sell them your old watch or they will smell your hesitation and pounce on you. If you push this step, forcing your watch over theirs, it will make them remember you forever. That is the key, remembering you. 'Cause each time you walk by them, they will look at you and know that you are the Kung Fu Master at Watch Selling... or Suit Selling (if you choose that angle instead).

Kung Fu Master in Hong Kong. And who doesn't want to be a Hong Kong Kung Fu Master?

Hey, that reminds me of someone. Bruce Lee! Shoot, you can be Bruce Lee! He was from Hong Kong, right? He fought all those people alone... kicking hundreds of people in duh face... looking them eye-to-eye... teeth littering the ground... big mess... being a Kung Fu Master like Bruce Lee... that would just be amazing...

Hummmmmm...

I wonder if he had a fake watch or tailored suit?

If he didn't, I bet I could sell him my old battered ones!

HIIIIIYAAHHHH!

# Modern Chinese Torture

When I was a kid, which my wife says was just yesterday, I was always duking it out with my younger brothers. If it wasn't because they didn't make my bed well enough (Hey, they were "younger" brothers... what did you expect?), it was because they cheated on a board game. Or wouldn't stop bugging me. Man, they were always bugging me too. It seemed like the only way to make them stop was to implement what we called "Chinese Torture Treatment."

Now everyone has heard of Chinese Water Torture, right? Person strapped to a board, a drip of water falling on his forehead... bloop... bloop... bloop. Well, I never got around to strapping my brothers to a board and rigging up a droplet contraption that would deliver the required torture, but I definitely delivered a wide range of punishments: thump on the chest, whack the back of their heads, or my favorite... wrestle them to the ground and do the "spit droplet" thing (you know... you pretend to spit a droplet of saliva from your mouth, then suck it back up... nasty, I agree, but a wildly effective psychological weapon on siblings). Everything we did to each other was dubbed: Chinese Torture.

As we grew older, my siblings and I slowly discontinued our Chinese torture on each other. The whole experience became tiresome and unoriginal. It wasn't until my family and I had arrived in China, that I realized the culture had not only kept the torture active and frequent, the Chinese also had developed a whole new variety. It could also all be targeted at me!

## Chinese Torture Technique #1: Sleeper Trains

"Get around China just like the locals... sleep in beds, wake up the next day and be at your wonderful destination." Sounds great, right?

They intelligently leave out the fact that you may be in a four person room with people who can snore so loud that the entire train vibrates on the tracks. If I hadn't witnessed it myself, I would call myself a liar. I'm not joking... it's something out of the Kung Fu movies... secret weapon stuff... need ear protection and a Get Smart "Cone Of Silence" to stop the noise. I mean, this guy needs some kind of Rhino Surgery. The girls, who were in the other room, could hear him.

Why is it Chinese Torture? Try nine hours of attempted sleep with this guy... nowhere to go... just your Alcatraz-sized bed and the other inmates struggling to keep our pillows from accidentally smothering this guy in his... Hey, how did this guy get any sleep anyway? Miracle.

## Chinese Torture Technique #2: Chicken Dishes

Before you go off on me, I'm a big chicken fan. Love Big Bird, Colonel Sanders, Tweety Bird. Big Fan. What I'm not a fan of is ordering a chicken dish and getting chicken parts. These are nice restaurants too, not some hawker stand in front of the train station. I'm talking about places with elevators and lights that work.

What do I mean by "Chicken Parts?" Let's see, how to do this and make sense. OK, you have a chicken, but the chicken meat, like the breast, the thigh, the drumstick is nowhere to be seen. What you have is spine bones with, what I think is, meat, random other bones, stuff that you can't chew or swallow without the Heimlich maneuver, and of course, my favorite, the feet. Chicken Parts!

Now I'm willing to bet that Chinese know a chicken has meat on it. You see chickens everywhere... everywhere... but where is all that meat going? It has to be going somewhere! An ancient Chinese secret, I'm positive. I also bet that if I figured it out, I wouldn't be able to leave the country.

Trying to eat Chinese chicken dishes were a clear form of paid torture. The cooks in the back are thinking "Hey, foreigners... make the Chicken Torture Dish... with the scraps in the back... see if they eat it... this is going to be SO funny. 10 Yuan says that the tall, skinny guy grins through the whole meal. This is going to be great!"

## Chinese Torture Technique #3: Smoke Inhalation

Anyone that has lived in Europe understands what it's like to be the "Designated Second-Hand Smoker." I felt like I was the only human on the continent that didn't smoke. "Is that dog over there puffing on a cigarette? Yeah, that one. Hey, I think it just flipped me off for staring!" Every day, it was my blessed honor of choking down others' fumes. In China, where there are over a BILLION people, that achievement comes with certificates of honor... like in college: "Summa Cum Laude Second-Hand Smoker awarded to..."

I'm not trying to be paranoid here, but it does feel like everyone happens to light up when you enter a room or closed space. Like an elevator. Or a bathroom. Or the train. Or an eight-seat tour bus. Though the driver was thoughtful enough to offer me a cigarette; points for sharing.

The torture comes not in this immediate moment, but in years to come. I could imagine my doctor's appointment when I returned to the States: "Mr. Jepson, there is good news and bad news. The good news is that your prostate is fine... (Thank Goodness I only have to do that every five years... I feel so violated!)... The bad news is your lungs and skin look like you puckered up to a diesel engine for twelve months. No worry though, with a diet of beets and boiled liver, you should regain a few months of your life back. See you in a year for your anal... I mean annual prostate check-up. Hehe... slip up there!"

So as you can see, China is not for the week of heart... or stomach... or sleep deprived.

The great thing was I felt like most of this stuff was solely in my head; that I could mentally overcome all of this so-called "torture." So what if my soup was a little grisly or crunchy? Who cares if I had developed a chronic cough? It was probably just pollution or radiation exposure. And finally, who doesn't have a relative that snores so loud that items mysteriously become missing around the house?

I mean it's only in my mind, right? The Chinese didn't seem to care... and there was like a billion of them.

Time for a little water droplet experiment to put things in perspective... Now where's that wooden board?

# You Know You're In China When...

Everyone has played the game, "You know you're wherever when..." No? You've never played this game? I thought everyone played this game. Oh well, you understand the basics, right? It's pretty self-explanatory by the title. It's great fun. Honest.

So let's start...

## You Know You're in China When...

You get honked at for being a pedestrian. Never in my life have I felt more like a player in the classic game "Frogger" than I did in China. Everyone wanted to run me over. It was not just the motorcycles, it was the cars, taxis, buses, police cars. Shoot, we almost got plowed over by an ambulance one day (if you're wondering, no siren or lights... they just wanted to get points by hitting us). At least we would have had adequate medical care with the ambulance... I think we would anyway.

## You Know You're in China When...

Honking your car horn is something of a sport. Since we are on the topic of honking horns, I've been curious to understand when and why someone honks their car horn. At first I thought honking your horn meant, "Get outta the way... Can't you tell I'm in a hurry?" just like it does in the States – a common and universal salutation, I thought. After being there a bit, I now believe it has nothing to do with being in a hurry 'cause China in the whole, is not in a hurry anywhere. Honking your horn, and I'm positive of this, means "Outta the way... I can't control this thing... Outta the way!" Pure panic. Since most Chinese just bought a car within the last few years, it has to be similar to having the whole road covered with teenage drivers. Total chaos and complete havoc! It's like putting 30,000 fifteen year olds in automobiles and telling them to all go crazy. It turns out to be an expensive crash-up derby.

## You Know You're in China When...

Your kids cry when it's time to get something to eat. Remember when you were a kid and your mom would tell you, "There are starving kids in China, don't waste your food." Little did I know it back then that it would be my kids that were starving in China. "Hey kids, let's go get lunch... (Smoke and the sound "Ziptang" - like looney tunes) Hey, where'd everyone go?" It's not that the food is that bad... OK, some of it is REALLY bad. It's just that so little of it is GREAT. Blame it on my ability to find a decent restaurant and actually order food. Maybe all of my Tarzan grunting made the Chinese think I'm so Cro-Magnon that I'd eat about anything.

## You Know You're in China When...

People ask to take pictures of you just because you're not Chinese. It was the kids, I understand that perfectly clear. Blond hair, blue eyes, cute smiles – They loved the girls, couldn't get enough of them. In a way, I felt the need to make up T-shirts with Chinese characters that say "Get a picture with my kids... 10 yuan." Make some money while we were at it. Maybe, I could have had them sing songs at the market. A trio of adorable American girls singing and dancing. Cindy and I with collection baskets. It may have been a million-yuan idea, which may be just enough to buy some really good food.

## You Know You're in China When...

Walking into a public bathroom is some type of horrific gas chamber. The fumes that were being generated would euthanize any small animal. "Ma'am, sorry about your dog; we just couldn't save him. We placed him in a Metro bathroom for five minutes to let him pass on." The only thing worse than having to do your business in a public bathroom in China is passing out, a complete lack of usable Oxygen pass out, from being in a public bathroom in China. The thought was so terrifying that it willed my mind into staying conscience. I know I have broken a few Guiness World Records for holding my breath; I just haven't gone to double check the record times.

## You Know You're in China When...

You think professional baseball players are pansies. Yes, I said pansies. One day in Beijing, I witnessed a grandma that spat a loogie that would have made any manly man impressed. There's a Chinese talent pool of loogie-spitters that is completely untapped. This same lady coughed up a cat and cracked a cement tile when she spat; if I hadn't been there I wouldn't believe it. Purely professional... decades of practice. I'm willing to bet she is so talented she could spat a pigeon off a branch from twenty paces. China is the loogie capital of the world and that's something special.

## You Know You're in China When...

There are more pre-packaged Ramen Noodle bowls in a grocery store than there are vegetables. Need something spicey, something green, something with seafood, something with chicken lard? OK, we didn't know if it was chicken lard but there were three packets inside the bowl. The seasoning was the powdery stuff... check. The vegetables were dehydrated and in small pieces... check. The last packet was a mushy, paste-like substance that we poked at for a few minutes and when it didn't bite us, determined it was alright to taste. Cindy thinks it was chicken lard with spices; a reasonable assumption. Me? I think it was chicken parts: the stuff that doesn't make it in the soup; stuff like guts, organs, eyeballs... stuff you have to grind up to sell.

And lastly, **You Know You're in China When...**

You feel like you're camping inside your hotel room. It's clean, yes. Towels, soaps, everything you need. It's the ply-board mattress and no heat that makes it more like camping than staying in a hotel. It's a tent on the 6th floor. It's better than camping in a few ways: a roof from the rain, doors to keep the rift-raft out, electricity... better. Sleeping in all your cloths to keep warm, seeing your breath when you're in bed, and having that "Oh, my back" pain from sleeping on concrete surfaces makes it feel more like camping.

And so you have it... life in China. It's an endless source of humorous adventures. You can't be there and not be amazed... yes, from loogie-spitting Grandmas to all the other impressive things and people. The unique experiences are truly endless and so is the lying...

Example: Time for lunch. How did I make them not hide from the thought?

"Come on kids, let's go get... er... ice cream. Yeah, ice cream!"

# What I Love About China

Culture shock. That was exactly what I had going to China. Could I have prepared myself more for the complete mental warfare I had in China? Maybe. Stew up my dog, stick my head in a smoke stack, try to read the words in a bowl of Chinese alphabet soup, build a few skyscrapers. Sure, I could have prepared better.

But why would I do something silly like prepare myself for the "True Chinese Experience;" the true "Shock of Culture" and its ugly cousin "Test of Wills." Why would I really prepare myself for the impact? It would dull the senses, it would lighten the adrenaline. That would be bad. You need to be smacked in the face with the culture shock, not softly slapped from a girlie boy. You need something... something like running really fast with your eyes closed and smacking into a brick wall. Of course it isn't smart, but it makes for great television and a memory you'll never forget. The experience is so deeply etched into the dark recesses of your brain you'll mutter the story to your grandkids through your oxygen mask.

And because I performed a swan dive into the subfreezing swimming pool of China, I can now relate to you, with all my frost bitten toes removed, what I love about China.

Applause for later please, it's hard to stand with only four toes on each foot.

I loved being pushed around in China. What do I mean by being pushed around? Well, at the Great Wall of China, the Forbidden City – anywhere of cultural significance – a mob of Chinese will push you and crowd you to get to where they are going. Cindy thought this was crazy; however, to me it was hilarious. I felt like I was in some mosh pit. Rock and roll! I even yelled out "Wheee!" once just because it was so entertaining. Who cares if it's not "acceptable" in other countries? If you think it's some amusement ride, you'll have just as much fun as I did.

I love Chinese Grandmas. These rugged ladies not only do the shopping, wash cloths in rivers, take care of the grandkids, they also form one of the best demolition groups in the world. Chinese grandmas can barge through any human obstruction with the expertise of the Kool-Aid Man. I've been physically removed from where I was standing by a Chinese grandma, and she couldn't have been taller than 4 feet 3 inches. Someone needs to start a Chinese Grandma Rugby league or something. It would be huge! Grandmas zooming around, blasting away other grandmas for the ball. Millions, I say Millions!

I love cabbage. If it wasn't for this vegetable, I wouldn't have eaten anything green for a month. Well, that's if you exclude all the things I couldn't recognize as food, or a vegetable for that matter. And, you can't count that one bread – that was just not natural. At least I thought it was bread. Man, what if it wasn't bread. Freak me out again like I freaked out from that meat we ate in Guilin. Still don't know what it was. Beef, pork, lung, kidney, dog. It's a toss-up. Anyway, I love cabbage, at least I think its cabbage. Gulp!

I love souvenir shops. For the first time in our world trip, the souvenirs that we bought in China, I could 100% guarantee, were MADE in China. It was so frustrating buying a trinket or gift in a country then look at the bottom and see it was made somewhere else – mainly China. We've even asked vendors if the product was made domestically and get a full-hearted "Yes," only to see the exact same item in the next country being sold as a local product there also. Finally, something locally made – like my Chairman Mao watch. "Hey, Mao stopped waving. I just bought this thing yesterday... piece of $#%^&!"

I love Chinese TV. There were basically three types of shows: the Chinese Soap Opera, the Chinese-Japanese War Soap Opera (it was not a documentary, the acting was way too cheesy), and the Chinese News Soap Opera (It was news with a Pro-China, Pro-Happy, Pro-Asia... did I say Pro-China yet?). Chinese TV was one of those miracle Chinese medicine treatments. It completely cured me of my male "Must-Have-Channel-Changer-In-My-Hand" condition. With almost nothing that I could understand or more importantly, anything that I could keep my attention longer than about ten seconds, I had hours more of my life available. It was fantastic. More time to ride the metro, buy steam buns, walk around and breathe the air (errr... I don't know if you can classify China's air as "air" – something to do with concentrations of ingredients).

I love Chinese Automobiles. Somehow, someway, I must get one of these cars sent to me here at home. For one, there is a brand of cars around China with a Star Trek symbol on the front. It's so funny. When you buy one of these autos, does it come with a solid red or solid blue crew-cut t-shirt? Do you have driver options of "stun" or "proton torpedoes?" Hilarious! I think I'm going to call my car "Excelsior," after the Centaur class of Star Trek spacecraft... er, why are you looking like that at me? No, I'm not a Trekkie... I just happen to know that stuff... by chance really... No, errr, yes, I have been to a convention... Only once though and it was for the comic books, not the Star Trek stuff. Honest!

I love Beijing Metro Station names. Yes, I'm at times childish, but you have to listen to some of these names. A good hand full of them reminded me of what my father used to say when he was totally ticked at me for breaking the back window or something similar. "Dengshikou" or "Dongsi" always made me giggle. How about "Dazhongsi," "Hui Long Guan," and "Taiyang Gong?" I loved saying them. Cindy gave me that motherly look of "Come on honey, it's not that funny." But she's a girl and doesn't get "Boy Humor." Say "Fucheng Men" like you're really mad and tell me if it doesn't make you bust out laughing.

There's so much to like about China. Sure, there was a crap-load of things to complain about because we didn't take an "American tour," but why not find the things that make you laugh or giggle a bit? Smiling is good for the face muscles. Giggling and laughing are good for the soul and mental health; calms you down, releases stress. Giggling and laughing are also good for the stomach muscles. Well, there are other things good for the stomach muscles too, but those are all culinary related.

Enough of that now... I think I'll go for a drive in "Excelsior" and test out that new horn I installed. Hits frequencies only Klingons can hear... and the occasional Chinese Grandma... though she's too busy doing a Captain Kirk karate chop (also known as "Kirk Fu") on someone, like in episode #46 "The Gamesters Of Triskelion"... man, Captain Kirk really gave that one guy a...

Er, it's totally coincidence that I know all that stuff...

Like, did you know that the new Star Trek Sulu was played by a Chinese-American Actor?

Totally coincidence that I knew that by the way! Coincidence, really!

# Chapter 10: Europe:

# Ahhh... Fresh Air at Last... Cough! Cough! Cough!

Humorous Insights

# London:  To Be or Not To Be Caffeinated

Kids' lives appear to revolve around when they can get the next sugar high.  My wife and I try really hard to keep our girls from bouncing off the walls but it can be hard when you are traveling and trying to keep them happy at the same time.  Sugar became the natural solution to taming the wild beast within our girls.

We discovered a few decent treats that could occupy them for a period of time and allow us parents to breathe for a second.  Suckers on airplanes and gum on long drives were miracle makers for keeping the bickering and whining to a minimum.  It was hard to argue with a plug in the mouth.  These items weren't always enough, as we found out in London.

We had an 18-hour, overnight layover in London before flying back to the USA.  We had two choices: go sleep in a hotel or drive around seeing the London sites.  We left the decision to the kids, seeing that they were getting older and had stronger opinions.

"How are we going to stay awake all night long?" asked our oldest.

"Well, I guess we could drink a lot of caffeine… like Coca-Colas or something." I replied.

Almost in unison, the girls started chanting "Coca-Cola! Coca-Cola!"  They were like recovering alcoholics who had accidentally fallen into a room full of Jack Daniels - eyes bulging, teeth bearing, drool pooling on the floor - so to avoid pitch forks and torches, we hesitantly agreed to the overnight drive-a-thon.

After getting the rental car, it was off to find the soda pop.  At 10:30 at night, all we found was a shady convenience store that had one of those attendants behind the bullet proof windows.  "Good," I thought, "at least I can get the soda."

So here's how the conversation went:

Me to cashier: "Hello, do you have Coca-Cola?"

Cashier (in a thick accent): "Yes... bleep bloop bleep bloop."

Me (now flustered because I thought this was England, where the English language had evolved and I didn't understand almost anything this guy was saying): "Coke? The soft drink Coca-Cola?"

Cashier (looking at me like I've got a Coke bottle up my...): "What size?"

Me (It's a miracle, he's cured): "Do you have medium sized bottles?"

Cashier: "Bleep bloop milliliters bleep bloop?"

Me: "Milliliters? I'm American... we drink it by the 'liter' not 'milliliter.' Give me five of the bleep bloop"

This he seemed to understand, and came back with five 550 milliliter bottles of Coke. He grinned and asked for fifteen pound, which was like 25 bucks at the time. So, this was the real plan. He mutters and distracts you until you find out you have had your pants ripped right off from under you.

Bleep blooping little bleep bloop! Good thing that smiling, little pirate was behind bulletproof glass, I wanted to kill him.

But then again, it was all for the experience... and experiencing our three daughters seeing London for the first time (that they remember), even though it was on a stimulant high, was well worth the price of beverages. And watching them crash after a whirlwind tour of the city, was a beautiful thing.

Peace and quiet for the fourteen hour plane flight while the girls slept it away - well worth 25 dollars of Coca-Cola - and once again proving that sugar is a parent's best friend. Though caffeine can be a close second.

## Pasqua is Pasqua!

Having lived in Italy for several years, when I go back, I find my knowledge of Italy to be very beneficial. Speaking Italian, understanding when Italians are making fun of me, eating lots of pasta, driving like a maniac and no one caring, and of course, understanding wacky Italian culture. This was particularly helpful when I happened to find myself in Italy during the traditional festival of "Pasqua," which translated into our simple tongue means "Let's eat for eight hours straight or until something more important happens, mainly a soccer game." Or, you can translate it as "Easter," whichever you prefer.

Sure, you're telling me that you understand what Easter is already. Well, let me tell you something. Easter is Easter, but Pasqua isn't really Easter... it's Pasqua! Yes, I know that Easter is Pasqua and Pasqua is Easter, and therefore Easter is equal to Easter, or simply put, Pasqua is equivalent to a whole number because anything divided by itself is one. Right?

But to an Italian it is more than just a holiday. It's spiritual. Spiritual enough to make the country stop watching soccer for ten minutes and find out where the closest cathedral is (ok, that's not that hard, but pulling an Italian away from watching soccer almost requires a Santa Maria sighting, which some have seen after Rome versus Milan games).

Italians view Pasqua as a holy day, but I would put it even more dramatic - Pasqua is like a Holy Crapoly holy day. Now that's Holy! Pasqua is also serious business in Italy, Christmas-type serious business. The whole country is decorated up with pastel colors. Window after window has the most beautiful display of...

Eggs?

Yes, eggs. The windows are filled with huge eggs. Chocolate eggs, plastic eggs, wooden eggs, ostrich eggs (don't ask me why ostrich

150

eggs, these are Italians we're talking about) and all are ENORMOUS! All decorated with scenes of... who cares, it's an egg. But it's an enormous egg.

Sure we have Easter eggs here in the States too, but eggs the size of the Pope's hat-thingy-thing? Shoot, in America the eggs are getting smaller not bigger. Last year alone, I believe I lost 20 Easter eggs in my backyard because they were so small no one could find them. I mowed up a good dozen the following week... jelly beans everywhere.

This brings me to why I mention this ENORMOUS Pasqua egg tradition. How on Earth can you have an Easter egg hunt if the eggs are so big you have to plant a bush in front of them to hide 'em?

Follow me here. Imagine, "Oh, I wonder if the kiddies are going to find the eggs this year? They found them last year and the year before... oh, let's just find out now. On your mark, get set, it's already over." Pow! It's over. The whole thing would last about as long as a Pop Tart in a diet seminar, but with fewer casualties.

I call it genius. No basket, egg too big. No losing eggs, just one big egg and not fifty million small ones. No green plastic grass. What is that crap anyway? No Easter bunny (how is that thing plopping out eggs anyway?).

Simply one big egg... and nothing else to bother you.

Now you're free to do whatever you want... like eat for eight hours or get back to watching soccer on TV.

Either way, it'll take the Santa Maria to pull me away from those things... and that would be ENORMOUS. Even for a Holy Crapoly day like Pasqua.

Forza Milan!

# Chapter 11:

# Closing Thoughts and Permanent Psychological Damage

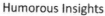

Humorous Insights

# Back to the Grind Called Work

Honestly... and I mean honestly, I was happy to come home. It had a lot to do with being with my wife and kids solid for 24 hours a day and seven days a week. Not for me though, I loved being with them. It was for them having to deal with *me* for all that time. They were ready to kill me. Only male in a group with four women, that was a time bomb ready to explode. I had detonated most of the landmines in that field and had survived most of them with minor concussions. I was playing with my life and the statistics weren't in my favor.

Also, after a year, I had lost credibility with them all. I needed time to build the house of cards back up. Such as:

"Dad, why do they use chopsticks?"

"'Cause they thought kids eat too fast with forks and they wanted to make sure their kids chewed properly."

"Dad, why do Australians drive on the opposite side of the road?"

"Well, they buy cars from Japan who drive on the left side and Australia is a British Commonwealth country, and the Brits like to do things completely different from the USA. But most importantly, water drains down the sink in a clockwise rotation above the equator and counterclockwise below the equator."

"Dad, are you making this stuff up?"

"Wow, look at the time... pack up, we're going home."

But more than anything else, I needed exposure to the fundamental of all North American creature comforts. College football? No, I mean I needed money (college football, may I highlight, requires money though). After waging currency war in every country we visited (the US Dollar treated us like a pimple on its forehead over that year), we needed moolah and we needed it fast. You understand, so that we could eat, have a roof over our heads, buy toilet paper - the three necessities of life, or at least that is how I remember them.

Sad to say that our trip ended because of money and not food poisoning, diarrhea, or that rash I developed on my arm (what is that and why do I crave wood chips?). That must be why money is the root of all evil. Evil dollar... EVIL! EVIL!

Life will never be the same. Or will it?

If I look now, it's very similar to what life was before the trip. I sit in my nice comfortable house, with my comfortable food, with my comfortable bed, and with my comfortable microsuede, fleece lined slippers... the ultimate definition of comfortable.

However, comfortable, I have to say, is boring.

Adventure is the spice of life (or is that basil?) and you have to have a spicy life, right? We're not talking black pepper spicy, we're talking Thai spicy. Otherwise, it's simple same-old, same-old comfortable.

I guess there are those that crave comfort - standard day, standard pay. I guess I was made from a different mold. I was wired differently. I guess I enjoy being a little on the edge, not knowing what life is going to pop up with next. If I had to choose what my autobiography would be, I would like the "choose your own adventure" book format. That's right. Where you start the book, decide on page 20 whether you want to "go to page 45 if you eat the noodle soup that is staring back at you with shrimp eyes" or "go to page 14 if you eat the meat dish from the lady with three teeth." Though if my recollection serves me correctly, choose your own adventure books always end with you falling to your death. Yep, that's right. Oh well, makes a good story.

It all boils down to choice. I want to choose my life and not have it dictated by someone else. To choose to live and experience serendipity. To choose to stand in an unfamiliar place, eat

154

unfamiliar food, sleep in an unfamiliar bed, and wear unfamiliar non-fleece slippers. To choose to be a little… uncomfortable.

There's a quote I love that I found when I got back, that's quite appropriate. It says:

> *"The best journeys answer questions, that in the beginning, you didn't think to ask."* Jeff Johnson, 120° South

Now that's some decent flavor.

Life is a journey but the best journeys, those that you don't know the conclusion to, are the memories that make it all worth the risk.

It all starts with deciding to be a bit uncomfortable and step out the front door and try something new and nonstandard. That's a step into the sunlight. And that's why I now tell my kids to "be quiet and eat your chicken feet."

Oooh! Spicy!

Made in the USA
Charleston, SC
19 January 2016